DATE DUE

Arranging Flowers for the Sanctuary

ARRANGING
FLOWERS

FOR THE SANCTUARY

Francis Patteson-Knight and
Margaret McReynolds St. Claire

with drawings by Francis Patteson-Knight

Foreword by The Very Rev. Francis B. Sayre, Jr.
Dean, Washington Cathedral

HARPER & BROTHERS, PUBLISHERS, NEW YORK

Library of Congress catalog card number: 61-6455

Dedicated with love and gratitude to Darrell, who patiently discussed the minor, as well as the major, points that arose in every chapter; and to Douglas, who suffered in silence.

Contents

Foreword

Francis B. Sayre, Jr.
DEAN, WASHINGTON CATHEDRAL

As long as men have lifted their hearts to the praise of God, flowers have adorned their sanctuaries. It may be a sprig upon a single grave, or an Easter garden set around the font in a great cathedral. But always the silent loveliness of nature's crown whispers of the Creator, reflecting the bountiful goodness that everywhere surrounds. "Let the whole earth stand in awe of Him," cries the Psalmist, for worship has ever been framed in the quiet beauty of holiness. Even the Puritans, sternly bare of distracting ornament, cleared away stained glass from the windows of their New England churches so that the woods and mountains and growing things could keep them company in their prayers. In the perfect handiwork of the Lord, man first discerns the image of his God, even as the changing seasons suggest the Providence that guides his destiny amid the uncertainties of life.

Besides, who is to say that worship is only words? Surely it is the whole of man that lifts his thanksgiving, awaiting God's blessing. Words are for his ears, thoughts for his mind—but flowers are for his eyes. A radiant part of the feast when a human soul communes with its Author!

A banquet is no better than the cook's recipe; this is no

less true of the feast with God. Much is entrusted to our hands, and if these hands are skilled, guided by patience and knowledge, then will our offering be worthy and the guests rejoice.

So was this book of hints born. Like the kitchen of some great castle, the nine altars of Washington Cathedral became a testing ground, a sweet-savored cuisine where new delights might be discovered. A pinch of this, and a dab of that, and lo and behold you have at last made something fit for the King.

In pursuing this worthiness, the authors have gone far afield—far beyond the precincts of the Cathedral where they began. I trust that the reader will follow their quest, retracing their steps in sanctuaries of their own, that wherever men gather to pray they may in truth behold the glory of the King.

> Who is this King of Glory?
> Even the Lord of hosts,
> he is the King of glory.

Preface

In recent years nearly every major flower show in the country has had at least one class with a religious theme. Specifications might call for altar arrangements for church or cathedral, for a special festival of faith, or simply for an arrangement with spiritual feeling. In fine, the exhibitors are called upon to present arrangements they would want to see in their own churches at Sunday services.

This book is presented as a help to those who will have the primary responsibility for their church decoration, now or in the future, and who wish their efforts to be as well designed as secular displays. We have aimed for a broad coverage of all aspects of church embellishment in accordance with not only the accepted principles of flower arranging, but also a church's design and the symbolism of the principal faiths.

The majority of the arrangements pictured in this book can be used as a guide not only for the altar but also for the home. It is our hope that each will serve to clarify the proper mechanics of arranging as well as to suggest what the arranger seeking improvements may accomplish on her own.

It is a privilege and an honor to prepare altars. It is also an act of worship.

F. P.-K.

M. M. St. C.

I

To Beautify the Place of My Sanctuary

> "The glory of Lebanon shall come
> unto thee, the fir tree, the pine tree,
> and the box together, to beautify the
> place of my sanctuary; and I will
> make the place of my feet glorious."
> (Isa. 60:13)

Architecture and Decoration

To a marked degree a church's architecture will dictate the decoration.

The conformation of windows, the breadth of the altar, the shadowed corners, all put their challenges and penalties on the arranger. Interior lines, in so far as they relate to any decoration, must be followed rather than canceled out. The successful arranger will complement the curve of the arches, the shape of the chancel, the wood or iron of the railings, with arrangements in which color and form are the two contributing factors. Every tree, every piece of plant material brought into the church must be in agreement with its background. There must be a union of design and purpose between the sanctuary and the flowers placed there to beautify it.

1

Not too many restrictions govern church decoration. But to follow the few that there are will bring deserved success.

Of first importance in Christian churches is the adornment of the altar. The cynosure is the Cross, and any arrangement put on the altar must not detract from its dominance or veneration. Vases used on the altar must harmonize with the Cross and the altar candlesticks. They cannot be so large nor so tall that the tops of the flowers interfere with painted or carved scenes above the altar. The cross sets the scale. All else is secondary and is governed by it.

Yet because arrangements in the sanctuary must be seen from a distance, the first care is to make any altar decoration bold and clear cut. Altar bouquets should have shape as well as mass. A security and strength of line and properly defined colors are necessary if a design's effect is to carry to the back of the church. Experience will tell the successful arranger when a display has character without violating its favored position in the church. The beauty of an altar arrangement is a tribute to the service. To be completely realized, however, it has to be appreciated by the farthest worshiper.

Elsewhere, as we have said, the church's interior style will control the setting of flowers and plants. There are not too many occasions when the arranger will wish to decorate within the congregation. On such days, though—at Christmas or Easter, for example—the church may be helped to acquire a greater glory. Sometimes on these occasions a greater amount of plant material is used. When there is enough space, growing plants or flowering shrubs may be brought in and placed against the walls. Additional candles with small pieces of foliage at their bases become motifs for the windows. A few wreaths, made, not bought, may hang in the foyer. Still, a select choice of simple materials is best. There is no time when good taste is not paramount.

A quick survey of any church will tell what decoration is most fitting for it. Generally the interior structure of countryside churches or of those more modern ones in the nation's growing suburbs accommodates itself best to the initiative of the arranger. The simplicity of small wooden churches, many of them constructed early in this century, emphasizes the beauty of any flowers placed to brighten a service. Similarly, the starkness of the latest churches and synagogues is accented remarkably by every bouquet, however small. The functional patterns of contemporary architecture have increased the personal rewards of church decoration.

Even so, not all arrangers work in contemporary surroundings. A substantial number are altar guild members of older churches, which have their distinctive lines and make their own demands. No two houses of worship are exactly alike. For the most part, and in modified forms, the older and larger churches in the United States come within four architectural classes—Byzantine, Romanesque, Gothic, and Renaissance. So many of them, however, are combinations of these classes that all but a few are difficult to categorize. While there are general rules for the adornment of each class, the arranger must still remember that each church has its own decorating problem.

The first of these, the Byzantine, was developed about A.D. 330 on the Bosporus and spread to other areas as the Empire grew. In this style the domes are rounded, the church has a great amount of brickwork, the interior art is somewhat lavish. The churches of St. Mark in Venice and

Sacré Coeur in Paris are typical of this style. Many Greek Orthodox churches in America follow the Byzantine manner. The Church of St. Agnes in Cleveland, Ohio, is an example. Because Byzantine interiors are colorful, the most successful arrangements utilize as much green material as possible. Cut foliage in different values of green or potted plants in planters combine very well with mosaics or stone. Arrangements in this type of church may be as large as the interior will permit.

The Byzantine period was followed by the Romanesque after A.D. 500, when the growth of papal powers gave new impetus to church building and increased popular enthusiasm and zeal for religion. Romanesque churches differed from the Byzantine in that they had thicker walls, small rounded arched openings, and groups of stories, towers, and vaulted ceilings. The greater portion of the cathedrals at Winchester in England and at Pisa in Italy are good illustrations. The Church of St. Bartholomew in New York City is constructed in this style. Arrangements for this type of architecture may use stronger, bolder flowers and heavier foliage. They should be either rounded at the top or fan-shaped to conform with the arched openings in such churches.

It is interesting that the word *Gothic,* used originally to denote contempt for the uncultured peoples of northern Europe, has become identified with the most typical style of Christian architecture. Cruciform in plan, complex in its units, Gothic architecture (from about A.D. 1100) has many modifications, but it always makes elaborate use of carved symbols and of stone, wood, stained glass, and marble as well as gilt. Notre Dame in Paris exemplifies the earliest complete expression of the style. Two excellent Gothic examples in the United States are the Washington

Cathedral in Washington, D. C., and the Cathedral of St. John the Divine in New York. With so much elaborate carving and often with a light or ornamented reredos, it is essential to frame the altar flowers quite deeply in green foliage. This is to insure that the arrangement will be visible from the rear of the building and that it be in harmony with its heavy surroundings. Also, on religious holidays small trees and evergreen branches can be effective in the broad reaches of these churches.

The baroque, or neo-classic, architecture called Renaissance (15th and 16th centuries) was copied from earlier Roman buildings and had its origin in Italy. San Carlo alle Quattro Fontane in Rome and the church at Escorial in Spain are good examples. For the most part this style is massive, with much use of gold, silver, simulated jewels, and embroidered paintings in the interiors. Some of the mission churches in the American Southwest are of this period. San Xavier outside of Tuscon, Arizona, is typical. The use of flowers is rather limited in these churches owing to the ornate decoration. Bouquets should be given frames of green, and cut material should be built up in depth as much as possible.

In this century and the last, hundreds of churches in the United States were built in the so-called Greek revival style. These are of wood and painted white. They are often galleried, the windows are clear glass, sometimes paned and fan-shaped at the top, and the interior is usually severe with white walls. At least one example can be found in most of the smaller cities of the country. In New England we find an example in King's Chapel, Boston. Such churches are among the easiest in which to arrange flowers. Greens and reds show well against their interiors. Their very plainness is an invitation to the arranger to embellish the glory of the service.

The modern Jewish synagogue is an outgrowth of the earlier Tabernacle and Temple. The Temple was called a sanctuary because it contained the holy Ark with the tablets of the Covenant, and only sanctified priests were permitted to enter the inner chambers. After the destruction of the Temple in A.D. 70, the synagogue replaced it as the sanctuary for the people.

The present-day synagogue is generally a rectangular building with the Ark at the eastern end opposite the entrance and with the almemar near by. Sometimes there are benches for men on either side, and a women's gallery may be reached by staircases from the outer vestibule. A combination of the almemar with the platform upon which the Ark rests is becoming general in American Reform congregations and on the Continent, but not in England. This combination has resulted in the elimination of certain Orthodox ceremonies along with the disappearance of open space around the almemar. It gives the congregation a better view of Ark, pulpit, and almemar.

The desire for greater viewing space has led to many variations in temple plans. In Temple Beth-El, New York, the seats are curved. Those at the side still face the Ark from parallel aisles. The same plan is used in the Temple in Indianapolis, but there the aisles converge.

The rectangular floor plan permits a simple treatment of the ceiling. It may be paneled, as in Shearith Israel Synagogue in New York, or it may be arched. The absence of a transept permits an unbroken surface, but there are instances of central domes or semidomes over the Ark.

The sanctuary of a synagogue is the area in which divine service is held. In this the Ark is the most important feature. It is usually decorated and raised on a platform which is reached by at least three steps and often by more. The almemar is a platform raised above the synagogue floor, whether in the center of the building or not. It is approached by steps, contains seats, and is surrounded by a railing.

In Reform congregations the men and women are never seated separately. In Orthodox congregations they are always separated, and in Conservative ones they may or may not be.

The pulpit from which the sermon is delivered may be on either side of the Ark, and occasionally it is in the center of the steps. In Maikve Israel Synagogue in Philadelphia the sermon is delivered from a desk on the almemar.

The modern synagogue has lost many traditional aspects in the search for abundant light, good acoustics, and comfort for the worshipers. Few emblems characteristic of the Jewish faith are allowable. Those permitted are interlacing triangles, the lion of Judah, and flowers and fruit forms. A perpetual lamp hangs in front of the Ark, and the tables of the Law surmount it. A seven-branched candelabra (called a Menorah) may be placed at either side. Hebrew inscriptions are seldom and sparingly used. Human figures are not used in stained glass windows.

Today building costs influence church and synagogue architecture. Churches in the contemporary styles are much less expensive to construct than ones in the Byzantine or Gothic manner. Contemporary churches and synagogues now employ a wide variety of glass, steel, and reinforced concrete in stylized, yet reverent, simplicity, along with many labor-saving devices. They can be raised in a relatively short time with modern construction methods, in contrast to the long hand-fashioned procedures of other years. Yet the churches do not violate the tradition of the ages. The high spires, the sharp roofs of the earlier forms are usually incorporated in the new designs.

Among flowers, the calla lily, amaryllis, strelitzia, and tulip are suited to modern design in both form and texture. Shades of orange, orange reds, and strong yellows show off to advantage with brass and copper. Calla lilies go well with a stylized reredos. True reds and blues and even tints of blue reds and blue pinks are excellent complements for silvered wood and metals, fieldstone, and limestone. Brick backgrounds will take more rustic arrangements, or odd ones, such as globe artichokes and squash.

Modern altars in contemporary churches are covered by liturgical cloths, yet the stress on their use, it seems, has decreased in recent years. The dorsal—the liturgical drape that hangs behind the altar—is of cloth and varies in color. For the most part, however, the use of liturgical cloths in the newer churches is confined to frontals, so-called because they hang over the front of the altar. The dorsals and frontals may be changed with the seasons, so the arranger will find new challenges to honor the spirit of the celebration. Seasonal flowers, particularly if they have bold shapes, can be used to offset the dignity of these altar hangings.

Small sanctuaries and altars will, in a sense, put more emphasis on the decoration of the space beyond the railing and within the congregational area. Perhaps realizing this, many architects have installed in such churches planters and recesses to accommodate them. Because there is often either so much color in their interiors or almost none at all, many excellent arrangements can be contrived with green foliage alone. This can include house plants, brought into the church for the day, cuttings, shrubs—in fact, anything living except small trees. Such plants as the philodendrons, dracaenas, and echeverias look well on pedestals or in planters. A row of plants under a plate glass window identifies it with the gardens outside. Yellow greens may be used where there is an abundance of yellow or orange shades on the woodwork. Against stainless steel, aluminum, or iron the blue and gray greens are most effective. Dark greens show best against gray or green mosaics.

Sometimes in buildings of the new style the arranger may stand for a moment in temporary despair. The walls and fixtures are matched in color schemes that need no further embellishment, the rich dorsals would overwhelm any arrangements placed before them, and the altar seems almost deliberately sparse and thin. Yet these same difficulties permit many striking effects. The height of an arrangement in relationship to the Cross is no longer important if the Cross is not set at the altar, but has instead been lifted as a grand symbol over it. In some contemporary churches there is a great deal of light, because the back and side walls are for the most part light-reflecting. These churches lack the baroque decoration and heavy tones of the older ones. If a short altar permits no more than one centerpiece, or not even that, other arrangements can be placed at the sides of the sanctuary, on pedestals or, with the permission of the clergy, on the floor. Not all the dorsals are of the traditional velvet. Some of the altar curtains are of a plain silk or neutral fabric, providing the exact contrast needed for a warm arrangement.

Symbolic Importance of the Altar and Its Accouterments

The Altar

The first altar mentioned in the Bible was erected by Noah after the ark touched dry land. According to a rabbinical legend, it was partly formed from the remains of an earlier altar built by Adam after he was expelled from Paradise.

Today the various Christian and Jewish churches leave the privilege of determining interior architecture and altar fittings to the individual church. In the Jewish temple the sermon is delivered from the pulpit. The Protestant and Roman Catholic churches have various names for the table from which the sacrament is served. They also have a pulpit and generally a lectern. The Scripture is read from the lectern, and the sermon is delivered from the pulpit. In small churches a single structure serves the purpose of both a lectern and pulpit.

The Sarum use (the customs of the cathedral and diocese at Salisbury, widely followed by other areas of the English church before the Protestant Reformation) are the source for this injunction: "Anything that does not pertain to the office should not be placed on the Altar."

There are two types of altar, the liturgical and the nonliturgical.

The liturgical, or free-standing, altar often has a shelf behind it. This shelf, which may be lower than or level with the top of the altar, is called a retable or gradine. It is upon the retable that the Cross, the candlesticks, and the containers for flowers are placed. There are, of course, exceptions, and sometimes the ornaments have to be placed directly on the altar.

The nonliturgical altar is not free-standing. It may have one or more retables. These are graduated like steps behind the altar. Since the retables may be higher than the top of the altar, care must be observed that the arrangements do not overwhelm the altar.

The altar may be of marble, stone, or carved wood. It may or may not have frontals. When a frontal is used, the hue of the flowers should complement its color and add to the beauty of the service.

When there is a Communion table, the Cross may be placed directly on the table. In many contemporary churches it is suspended or located above the table or altar.

If the Cross is suspended, side pedestals or wall niches may be used for the flowers. Flowers also may be placed on a small shelf directly beneath the Cross, so long as they do not interfere with the office.

A central pulpit, such is as found in many Protestant churches and in Jewish synagogues, is best treated with either a pair of tall containers or with arrangements on pedestals, one on each side of the pulpit or reading desk. The shape of the arrangements should be either a vertical or a triangular mass. The tops of the flowers should never be as tall as the top of the pulpit or desk. Some churches have a table placed below the pulpit, on which flowers may be placed. In this instance an arrangement more horizontal than vertical is appropriate. It should extend high enough to be seen from the far end of the church, but it should not detract from the service by either its beauty or the lack of it. The arranger may try for striking and dramatic effects, knowing that the advanced architecture of the church will keep these designs in good taste.

Generally contemporary churches either tend to a strict austerity inside and out or have been made colorful with all the skills of present-day art. The lines are economical, and all detail not needed for the ritual has disappeared. Some churches are rectangular in form, others are circular, and still more have the conventional long aisles of the classic styles rising from the chancel through a fan-shaped auditorium.

The more austere churches are almost monastic in design. They are usually built of field or natural stone, tinted concrete, or brick or of one of the American woods, of which redwood is the most popular. Their altars are equally severe and are often made of the same material as the walls. The chancel rails are often wrought iron or steel; the roofs are planked and polychrome; the altar fittings reflect the conventions of modern sculpture. At the same time the lighting conditions have improved over former years. With better electrical fixtures or with plate glass windows for walls, the interior illumination in many of these churches almost approaches daylight. Contemporary churches have a freedom and spaciousness not found in the classic structures. There is a new joy in their stone sculpture, their wooden Crosses, their mosaic murals, and their enameled or copper reredos, that places these churches squarely in their functional age. Their congregations, by being raised above the chancel or brought nearer to it, have a sense of closer participation in the service. The absence of interior detail glorifies the ever-present Cross.

When the Cross is placed directly on a Communion table or altar, great care must be taken that it remains the dominant object. The flowers are there to enhance and point up the Cross. Simple greens, well arranged, may often be used with good effect and give added importance to the altar.

The Cross

The cross is one of the oldest and most widely used symbols in Christianity. There are over fifty forms of the cross. The most common types are the Greek and Latin, crosses, which may be made of silver, brass, or wood.

The Greek cross has four arms of equal length. It is often

used on church furnishings, silver, and fair linens. It is either carved, engraved, or embroidered.

The best-known cross is the Latin one, upon which Christ was crucified. An interesting legend is related to it. At Adam's death Eve was instructed by the Archangel Michael to plant on the grave a branch from the tree of knowledge. The branch grew and flourished, and the tree was still standing when Solomon started his Temple. He ordered the tree cut to be used as a pillar, but when its size was found unsuitable, it was discarded. Later it was used as a footbridge; when visiting Jerusalem, the Queen of Sheba noticed the miraculous quality of the wood and warned Solomon that from it a cross would be built. This cross, she said, could destroy the Jewish people. The wood was thrown into the Pool of Bethesda where it floated away and was lost. Later, as the queen had predicted, it was found, stored, and used for Christ's crucifixion.

Of the more than fifty forms of cross, the most frequently seen is the Latin cross. It is the cross found on Protestant altars and generally stands on three small steps, which represent love, faith, and hope.

A plain, or empty, cross is generally used in Protestant churches. Sometimes the plain cross carries the symbols of the four Evangelists upon its arms, with the lamb, symbol of victory, marking the crossing. Or it may have five red jewels or marks upon its face representing the five wounds that Christ suffered upon the Cross.

The crucifix, or cross with the figure of Christ crucified, is symbolic of the death of Christ as a complete sacrifice for our salvation. This is often used in the Lutheran Church during the Lententide or Passiontide to emphasize the season prior to Easter and the Ascension of Christ. The Roman Catholic Church always uses the crucifix. This cross with Christ on it is symbolic of His sacrifice and the self-sacrificing life of the Christian ideal.

The Gothic cross is often seen in contemporary churches. Within the arms of this cross is a circle that represents "life without end."

Lights

Light, in the form of either lamps or candles, has always had an historic importance in religious services.

The Word in the Scriptures is symbolized by either a lamp or a light. There is an early reference in the Bible to the Temple candlesticks, and since it does not describe them, they are assumed to be of a shape common in the homes of the times. The Rabbin (the authoritative Jewish source on law and doctrine) states that when the robes of the priests became unfit for wear, they were unraveled and the material was employed as wicks for the sacred lamps.

Religious lamps date back to Egyptian and Greek times and were in early use at the first shrines of Christendom. It was not until the twelfth century that candles made their appearance in the chancel or on church altars. Even then there was no uniformity in their size, number, or usage.

Since electricity is now used throughout the church, candles in the sanctuary are more symbolic than functional. Two candles are used in Protestant churches. These are symbolic of the divine and human natures of Christ. One is placed on each side of the Cross. In the Episcopal Church these candles are referred to as "eucharistic lights" and are lit only for a Communion service.

A candelabra with three candles is symbolic of the Holy Trinity. Six white lights represent the six days of creation.

In the Roman Catholic Church six candles stand for the church's round of prayer. Six candles are also lit for a solemn Mass. Seven are used when a pontifical Mass is sung by a bishop in his own diocese. Four are used at a bishop's private Mass, and two at all other Masses.

For the Mass, the flower containers are placed between the candlesticks, though not too close to them. They should not be so imposing as to dominate the candlesticks, which are part of the church fittings. The best containers are ones that seem inconsequential, yet maintain quiet harmony with all else around them.

A seven-branched candlestick represents the Old Testament worship, the Church and the seven gifts of the Holy Spirit. The Jews call it Menorah, and it is common in synagogues today. It is generally electrified now and is used more for ornamentation than as part of the religious service. Reform Jews, however, light two candles at their Sabbath service and on religious holidays. While the Orthodox and Conservative Jews do not have candles burning in their synagogues, they light at least two in their homes on the night of the Sabbath. They may light an additional one for each child if they so desire.

The Festival of Lights, one of the lesser Jewish feasts, which has been celebrated for more than twenty-one hundred years, commemorates a historical victory. This was Judas Maccabaeus' freeing of Jerusalem and his clearing the Temple of the Syrian pagan idols. The Hanukkah service held in synagogues today celebrates that victory and includes a light ceremony and the chanting of the Al Ha-Nissim.

In Roman Catholic and some Protestant churches, besides the candles, there are sanctuary lamps, which are kept burning all the time. Usually these lamps have red glass shades and are made of metal in a wide variety of designs to harmonize with the architecture of the church. They are filled with beeswax or olive oil which has a floating wick. The union of fire and oil is said to be symbolic of a link between Christian worship and the Old Testament. It also denotes the unseen presence of Jesus Christ in the church.

Vestments

From early times, distinctive dress has dramatized the medicine man, the soothsayer, and the priest. The word *vestment* is from the Latin and signifies simple clothing. It now refers to the garments worn by ministers of religion in the performance of their sacred duties.

In the Jewish religion every detail of the vestments once was specified very carefully. The Jewish people had such high veneration for the vestments of the high priest that a lamp was kept constantly burning before the repository of the sacred robes. Now the rabbi and the cantor wear the daily dress of the male members of the congregation. In Reform congregations rabbis often wear a robe. It has no religious significance, and its use is entirely a matter for the individual synagogue to decide.

Presumably the clergy wore the common dress of laymen during the first four centuries after Christ, as there is no record of any special garb for them. Since all men wore long and flowing garments at that time, the vestments for divine service probably took this form.

In the present-day Roman Catholic Church five colors —white, red, green, violet, and black—are generally used for sacred vestments. A sixth color, rose, is used for solemn Mass on the third Sunday in Advent and on the fourth

Sunday in Lent. Also gold may be substituted for white, red, or green.

Each of the five liturgical colors has its special significance.

White symbolizes purity, innocence, or glory. It is used on the feasts of our Lord and Blessed Virgin, on festivals of angels, and for all saints who were not martyrs.

Red is symbolic of fire and blood. It will be seen at Masses on Pentecost and at feasts of all saints who were martyrs and shed their blood for their faith.

Green signifies growth and the increase in the Church. It is also symbolic of hope. Green is used on days other than Saints' days.

Purple, or *violet*, is for penance. This is the color prescribed during Lent or Advent, except on saints' days and on the festival of the Holy Innocents.

Black mourns the dead and is used at all requiem Masses for the dead and on Good Friday.

The vestments worn by the clergy at the Roman Catholic Mass correspond with the schedule of liturgical colors. Vestments are rarely worn by the Protestant clergy in America, with the exception of the Episcopal and Lutheran clergy. The colors closely correspond with those worn by the Roman Catholics. Generally, Episcopalian priests and bishops and some Lutherans wear surplices and other articles of clerical clothing. The trend today in Protestant churches is toward wearing robes. Ministers have found that robes help worshippers to focus their attention on the religious messages. Vestments are visual aids to worship, in harmony with church tradition. Used in good taste, they add dignity and formality to a service.

The black gown is generally accepted now for most Protestant churches. This is a long, full robe with full sleeves and loose-fitting collar. It is usually of heavy silk or serge. Some have white tabs, which represent the two tablets on which the Old and New Testaments were written. The stole, usually worn with robes, symbolizes the yoke of obedience to the Master. Often a minister has five stoles, which he wears according to the liturgical colors of the Christian year.

It is highly essential for one in charge of the flowers at a church to know the color of the vestments to be worn and the liturgical colors to be used, so a harmonious unit may be produced. Since the vestments and the altar frontal are not always the same color, the arranger may find an additional problem in creating a congruous whole.

Progress of the Service

Certain places in a church *must not* have flowers or adornment. Simplicity and restraint are always preferable to overdecoration. In many parts of the sanctuary floral arrangements will interfere with the progress of the service.

Most altars are too narrow to hold flowers without their conflicting with the service. Thus, many denominations have the unwritten rule that flowers must be kept from the altar.

No flowers are permitted in front of the Tabernacle or upon the Tabernacle. The altar rail must not be decorated at a time when it would interfere with the communicants.

Plants or vases of flowers placed on the chancel steps may lead to an accident. The priest or minister often finds it distracting, and perhaps hazardous, if the hand rail that leads to the pulpit or the pulpit shelf is adorned with plant material.

There are also other spots where decoration is not

appropriate from an esthetic viewpoint rather than because of interference with the service. These would include carved pillars of choir stalls and fine stained glass windows.

There will be times when services are held in two or more parts of the church. It creates a pleasing harmony if the same color or variety of flower is used at both. If services are to follow one another in different chapels, a small movable planter can be useful. Thus, one pair of arrangements can suffice for more than one chapel or service.

II

In the Fellowship of the Church

The Layman's Role in the Church

Beginning with the New Testament, the layman in the Church has had his place and his role in Christianity. His faith and gifts have insured the survival of the Church from its founding, in part through the building of places of worship that have been his refuge, his sanctuary, his comfort, his place of baptism and death. As each church required more and more beauty, more accouterments, the layman undertook in greater measure the financial responsibility for its proper care.

Into this area the women have moved with various duties, not the least of which has been the preparation and beautification of the altars and the chancels each Sunday. Their lay activity of arranging the flowers has taken many hours of care and devotion.

Traditions of Decorating Places of Worship

Flowers have been used in religious worship since the earliest times. The ancient Egyptians decked their temples with cut flowers. Frescoes that have been preserved show vessels filled with lotus buds and blossoms being carried in procession. The lotus was dedicated to the goddess Isis. This flower motif appears time and again throughout the course of Egyptian art.

On the other hand, there is an almost total absence of flower bouquets in vases of ancient Greece and Rome. Here the custom of fashioning wreaths and garlands predominated. Many professional workers were engaged in the making of garlands and wreaths for use in everyday life. Garlands were awarded to victorious soldiers and athletes, conferred on scholars, worn by statesmen, or exchanged by lovers. A wreath hung from the door of a house proclaimed the birth of a son. Extravagant garlands decked the statues of gods and goddesses and adorned sacrificial animals. Scarves filled with fruits and flowers were placed before statues of the gods. From this custom came the swag, a decorative motif seen in neo-classic architecture.

We know the month of May was dedicated to the Roman goddess Flora. At this time of year Roman children made clay statues and hung them with flowers. These crude May dolls symbolized spring and were probably the forerunners of Easter statues in the primitive Christian religion.

The early Christian Church realized quickly it would be easier to establish a new religion among an illiterate people if its signs, symbols, and established holidays were adapted from pagan use. Accordingly, the month of the pagan goddess Flora soon became May and our month of the Christian Mary. Saturnalia, the feast of Saturn, preceded the winter solstice. Gradually this season became associated with the birth of the Saviour and the glorious tidings of Christmas.

Flowers were also a part of religious worship in the East. We have detailed accounts of their use as early as the sixth century A.D. In accordance with their doctrines against the taking of life, the Chinese Buddhists were reluctant to cut flowers. Instead, they used flowering plants upon their altars. Written evidence exists that buds and blossoms, placed in what were probably ceremonial wine beakers, were used in the temples during Tang Dynasty, A.D. 618-906. When the missionary Buddhist priests went to Japan, they took with them large bronze vases for floral offerings. By this time they had developed methods for prolonging the life of flowers. Their arrangements, called "Rikka" (there are several spellings of the word), were constructed of flowers, evergreens, and bare branches and were very large and complicated. Judging by accounts left by Buddhist priests, we find they were often fifteen feet high. Some of them took several days to complete.

The Old Testament has many references to floral decorations. There is a reference to the Feast of Booths, where the Sukkah is used, in Leviticus 23:40-43:

And ye shall take you on the first day the boughs of goodly trees, branches of palm trees, and the boughs of thick trees, and willows of the brook; and ye shall rejoice before the Lord your God seven days. And ye shall keep it a feast unto the Lord seven days in the year. It shall be a statute forever in your generations: ye shall celebrate it in the seventh month. Ye shall dwell in booths seven days; all that are Israelites born shall dwell in booths: That your generations may know that I made the children of Israel to dwell in booths, when I brought them out of the land of Egypt: I am the Lord your God.

In the Book of Nehemiah 8:15-18, instructions are given for the building of these booths, which had been used since the days of Joshua, son of Nun.

The Feast of Succot was a harvest thanksgiving and has remained so through the centuries. The Sukkah which is featured at this festival is a frail building, with boughs laid across the timbers to form a roof, through which one can see the sky and stars. The decorations include fruits and foliage hung from the supports.

Four plants occupy a prominent place in the Succot festival.

1. Arravan. "Two willow branches which have neither beauty or fragrance." They stand for the man who neither knows the Law nor does any good deed.

2. Hadassah. "Three twigs of myrtle," having fragrance but no beauty to the eye, resembling a man who does good work without any knowledge of the law.

3. Lulab-Palm shoot. This represents the man who knows the Law but fails to apply its precepts to his living.

4. Ethrog. A citrus fruit, "both lovely and fragrant," the symbol of the man who knows the law of God and keeps it.

Another festival of the Jewish faith with an agricultural connection is Shanvuot. At this time both the house and the synagogue are decorated with flowers and green plants.

Today in Palestine men, women, and children can be seen on Friday afternoons carrying flowers for religious decoration. Florists are permitted to remain open later so that everyone has an opportunity to participate in this new custom.

From the beginning of the fourth century in Europe, when the Emperor Constantine had established Christianity as the state religion, buildings were set aside for worship. As time went on and the Christian faith took a firmer hold, the spiritual significance of church architecture and ornaments became greater. In 1295 Durandus, Bishop of Mende, recommended that growing plants supplement the ritual of the Church. Flowers in general were considered emblems of goodness.

The practice of placing garlands before the statues of saints and on candlesticks was pursued fairly consistently until the eighteenth century. In England, for instance, reference is found to garlands and wreaths worn and carried by the choir and the clergy. Churches were strewn with sweet-smelling herbs. Today some churches still practice the custom of crowning the Virgin Mary or the Christ Child with fresh flowers.

During the Middle Ages in England, the sacristan's garden was devoted to plants to be used in the church. St. Mary's Garden in the monastery grounds at Melrose Abbey in Scotland shows that there must have been some definite connection with the church. Just how the plants were put to use is not told. Probably the foliage plants and blossoms were used for garlands and the herbs for strewing.

Fruits and flowers were introduced in Renaissance churches and art. New interest in the literature of the ancient Greeks revived the classical love of nature. Swags and garlands were used extensively at that time. These were fashioned of flowers, fruits, and pine cones. Flowers also were used in vases as decorations during the Renaissance, but no paintings show flowers on the altars. Flowers were tolerated near the altar rather than encouraged and were probably placed on the floor of the sanctuary.

During the last century the use of flowers in the church has become more widespread, and it is now an accepted thing to find flowers within the sanctuary. They are either on the retable, on pedestals, or in planters. On special occasions more elaborate decorating its often undertaken, and here the women of the congregation have stepped in and taken on the arranging of the flowers. They have usually established a flower committee, and from these committees altar guilds have developed.

The Flower Committee

Depending on the size and locality of the church, the committee in charge of the flowers and/or linens may be set up in several ways.

When the congregation is small or in a rural area, it is often wise to assign one or two women for a month's duty at a time. Additional help may be obtained at the time of festivals, when extensive decorating will be undertaken. In large city churches and cathedrals, where there is often more than one altar to prepare and where a number of services are held weekly, it is advisable to set up the committee in detail.

At the Washington Cathedral in Washington, D. C., the following system has been working smoothly for some time.

The general chairman of the altar guild heads two separate groups, the linen committee and the flower committee. The linen committee is responsible for the preparation of the altars and the care of the linens. This group is also responsible for the laundering and repairing of the linens.

The flower committee is necessarily large because of the nine altars to be decorated. However, on a normal Sunday, flowers are placed on only four altars. This committee consists of a chairman who works closely with the general chairman of the altar guild, with whom she discusses the budgets for each Sunday's flowers, memorial flowers, and the flowers for special services. They also go over proposed designs sketched by the chairman for the festivals.

The flower committee chairman is assisted by an executive committee of three. One is the buyer and has contact with the florist. After checking the church calendar, and asking the florist about the availability and prices of flowers, she discusses with the flower chairman what colors are to be used for the various altars. The buyer places her order early in the week for delivery Friday. A book kept by the flower buyer, listing the variety, color, and price of each week's flowers, has proved invaluable over the years. This book not only shows exactly how much money has been spent but is also an easy calendar to follow for which flowers are most readily available at certain times of year. It is also a record of what has been ordered for past festivals.

Another member of the executive committee is in charge of supplies—the scissors, wires, Twist-ems, and other items used by the arrangers. She sees that all the necessary tools are available. She puts in requests for new supplies to the flower chairman, who sees that they are ordered.

The third executive committee member is in charge of housekeeping. This consists of seeing that there is water in the vases on the altars during the week, of removing vases of spent flowers from the altars, and of seeing that the vases are clean and ready for the workers who will arrange the flowers on Saturday, and that all vases not in use are carefully put away. She makes certain that all containers are filled with water and in place when the florist makes a delivery. She is responsible for discarding spent flowers and foliage. She sees that the sacristy is kept clean, with everything in its proper place, and that each week the supplies are checked.

The remainder of the flower committee is divided into six teams by the chairman. Each consists of five workers with a captain in charge. Each team works one week out of every six and is on call from Saturday morning until the following Friday afternoon. It handles the decorating of the cathedral for any service that may be scheduled during the time it is on call, whether wedding, funeral, or some special service. The captain alerts her workers for extra duty and is responsible for the sacristy's being left in order after the arranging is finished.

One member of the executive committee is on call for a month at a time, and if the captain of the week finds that her team is short-handed, she calls that executive committee member to fill in.

For the great festivals of Christmas and Easter the whole flower committee is on hand. The work is assigned ahead of time at a meeting at which the executive committee and the captains are present and when the decorating of each altar is discussed. At the same time it is determined what flowers and how many will be used, and the names of those responsible for the arranging on particular altars are selected

The decoration of a church, of course, is not as complex as that of a cathedral. Parts of this procedure may, however, be adopted by the altar guilds of the larger churches.

Contacts with Florists

Today the commercial growing of flowers has reached such a high standard that many beautiful flowers are available from the florist all through the year.

Most florists are willing to cooperate in providing exactly

the desired stage of opening, from bud to full bloom. Experience dictates that the better practice is to make a contact with one florist and give him all of the church orders. Not only will he become familiar with the quantities needed each week but he will know how deliveries should be made and at what time.

It is most important to have the flowers delivered to the church and left somewhere out of a draft and sun. They should be left in large, deep containers which have been filled with water and are exactly where the flower committee expects to find them. On each delivery, be sure the invoice is taken off the flowers and carefully checked. This should be kept by the arranger to hand over to the altar guild head or to the person paying the church accounts. It is advisable to check with the florist each week to find out what plant materials are available and thus avoid disappointment. Discussions of prices at the same time will save the altar guild many extra costs.

Remove any wire, string, or rubber bands holding flowers together if they are to be kept overnight before arranging. Roll the flowers in newspaper, and immerse paper and stems in deep water. This keeps the flowers upright, helps strengthen the stems, and protects them from sudden changes in temperature.

Memorial Flowers

Each Sunday many churches have flowers donated by their members for services in memory of the dead. In some instances the church places a limit on the amount that may be spent for such arrangements. This is especially wise in the small church, where a person would feel more free to sign up for a donation if he knew the cost limit in advance.

It is necessary that the person giving the flowers discuss them with some responsible member of the flower committee. The flowers must be of the correct color when liturgical colors are used. If possible, it is best to order the flowers from the florist generally used by the church. He will know the delivery entrance of the church and the proper procedure in their disposition so that they will remain in the best possible condition. If the money is given to the altar guild or the flower committee, one of the regular members may arrange the memorial flowers. In practice this has been found to be a more efficient procedure.

When this is not possible, either because the donor wishes to arrange them herself or wishes to supply them from her garden, then she should be advised to use spike and round forms. Flowers of these types lend themselves to more pleasing arrangements and are nearly always sure in their effect.

Flowers from many sanctuaries are taken to the sick after the service. When this is done, care in the choice of flowers is important. The blooms should have lasting qualities. In the church a stem has to be cut to make the flower conform with the design, but this does not mean that the flower has been ruined for the arrangement for the sick. All arrangements need flowers with different stem lengths. It is often possible to save the florist's papier-mâché containers. These can be kept at the church and used for delivering arrangements to the sick.

III

O Let Winter and Summer Bless Ye the Lord . . .

BOOK OF COMMON PRAYER
Benedicite, Omnia opera Domini,

Christian Calendar

The Christian, or church, calendar is arranged according to the seasons and festivals of the church. The year begins with Advent, the season which precedes the festival of Christmas. This calendar is based on the observances in the Protestant and the Roman Catholic year. Since altar hangings and vestments of each liturgical color are selected, flowers should be planned with reference to this schedule.

Date or nearest Sunday		*Day or Season*	*Liturgical Color*	*Duration of Season*
	ADVENT		violet rose (Roman Catholic)	4 Sundays
November	30	St. Andrew	violet	
December	21	St. Thomas	red	
	CHRISTMAS SEASON		white	1 or 2 weeks
	24	Eve of Nativity	white	
	25	Christmas	white	
	26	St. Stephen	red	
	27	St. John the Evangelist	white	
	28	Holy Innocents	red	
January	1	Circumcision of our Lord	white	
	EPIPHANY		white green (Episcopal)	2-6 weeks
	6	Epiphany and the octave of Epiphany	white	8 days
	25	Conversion of St. Paul	red	
February	2	Presentation in the Temple	white	
	24	St. Matthias	red	
		Pre-Lenten Sunday (Lutheran)	green	
	EASTER SEASON—LENT		violet	46 days
46 days before Easter		Ash Wednesday	violet	
March	25	Annunciation	white	
		Fourth Sunday in Lent (Roman Catholic)	rose	

Date or nearest Sunday	*Day or Season*	*Liturgical Color*	*Duration of Season*
Sunday before Easter	Palm Sunday	violet	
	Holy Week	violet	6 days
	Good Friday in Holy Week	black or no paraments	
	Holy Saturday in Holy Week	white (Vespers)	
	Easter and its octave	white	8 days
	Eastertide	white	5 weeks or 50 days
April 25	St. Mark	red	
May 1	St. Philip and St. James	red	
40 days after Easter	Ascension and the Sunday following	white	2 days
50 days after Easter	Pentecost and Monday in Whitsuntide	red	2 days
First Sunday after Pentecost	Holy Trinity and the octave of the Holy Trinity	white	8 days
	TRINITY SEASON	green	22-27 weeks
June 24	Nativity of St. John the Baptist	red	
29	St. Peter and St. Paul	red	
July 2	Visitation	white	
25	St. James the Elder	red	
August 6	Transfiguration	white	
24	St. Bartholomew	red	

Date or nearest Sunday		Day or Season	Liturgical Color	Duration of Season
September	21	St. Matthew	red	
	29	St. Michael and All Angels	white	
October	18	St. Luke	red	
	28	St. Simon and St. Jude	red	
Sunday preceding October 31		Reformation Day (Protestant)	red	
November	1	All Saints, and Sunday following	red	2 days
Fourth Thursday in November		Thanksgiving	red white (Episcopal)	

Jewish Calendar

The Jewish calendar, which is based on the period from one new moon to the next and on the condition that neither Rosh Hashana nor Yom Kippur may fall on the day before or the day after the Sabbath, has six different lengths of year, with 353, 354, 355, 383, 384, and 385 days. The Jewish year generally has twelve months, but sometimes adds a thirteenth, called Veadar. Every nineteen years the Jewish year coincides with our civil year, give or take a day or two.

The Christian calendar is closely related to the civil calendar, with the exception of Easter, which is determined by the moon. Generally Easter and the week of Passover coincide. In some Jewish leap years Nisan 1 falls so late that Passover occurs a month after Easter. Hanukkah and Christmas approximate the same date every two or three years.

The chief holidays in the Jewish religious year are: Rosh Hashana, Tishri 1; Yom Kippur, Tishri 10; Sukkoth, Tishri 15 to 21; Shemini Atsereth, Tishri 22; Passover, Nisan 15 to 21; Shabuoth, Sivan 6 and 7. These are all observed by the Reform, Conservative, and Orthodox Jews. Rosh Hashana may occur between September 5 and October 4. The first day of Hanukkah may be between November 27 and December 27, and the first day of Passover between March 26 and April 25.

Hanukkah (8 days) and Purim are half-holidays observed by all, but the Conservative and Orthodox congregations add Shushan Purim. At the time of the holidays no fasts are observed by Reform Jews. It is not necessary to use any specific color for a religious festival observed by Orthodox, Conservative, or Reform Jews.

The months of the Jewish year with the principal religious holidays observed by all Jews are as follows:

Month	Day or Season	Length
Tishri	1 Rosh Hashana (New Year)	
	10 Yom Kippur (Day of Atonement)	
	15 First Day of Sukkoth	7 days
	22 Shemini Atsereth	
Heshvan		
Kisler	25 Hanukkah	8 days
Tebet		
Shebat		
Adar	14 Purim	
Nisan	15 First day of Passover	
	21 Seventh day of Passover	
Iyar		
Sivan	6 First day of Shabuoth	
Tammuz		
Ab		
Elul		

Growing Seasons

The blooming periods of flowers vary with the section of the country, but the following list may act as a guide. Check your local conservation list and, if any of these plants are on it, do not use them unless they are judiciously pruned from home yards.

White

SPRING	SUMMER	AUTUMN	WINTER
Amaryllis	Agapanthus	Aster	Camellia
Calla lily	Amaryllis	Buddleia	Chrysanthe-
Camellia	Buddleia	Camellia	mum
Cyclamen	Carnation	Chrysanthe-	Helleborus
Daffodil	Daisy	mum	(Christmas
Delphinium	Geranium	Cyclamen	rose)
Gardenia	Gladiolus	Dahlia	Poinsettia
Hyacinth	Hydrangea	Gladiolus	Rose
Iris	Ismene		
Larkspur	Petunia		
Lilac	Phlox		
Magnolia	Rose		
Madonna lily	Snapdragon		
Peony	Zinnia		
Ranunculus			
Rhododendron			
Tulip			
Virburum			
Rose			

Red

Anemone	Amaryllis	Aster	Chrysanthe-
Hyacinth	Coxcomb	Chrysanthe-	mum
Peony	Day lily	mum	Poinsettia
Ranunculus	Geranium	Coxcomb	Rose
Rose	Gladiolus	Dahlia	
Tulip	Phlox	Gladiolus	
	Rose	Rose	
	Snapdragon		
	Zinnia		

Pink or Rose

SPRING	SUMMER	AUTUMN	WINTER
Camellia	Amaryllis	Aster	Camellia
Hyacinth	Geranium	Camellia	Chrysanthe-
Hydrangea	Gladiolus	Chrysanthe-	mum
Kalmia	Petunia	mum	Cyclamen
Larkspur	Phlox	Dahlia	Rose
Peony	Rose	Gladiolus	
Rhododendron	Rubrum lily	Rose	
Rose	Snapdragon		
Tulip	Stock		
	Zinnia		

Blue

Delphinium	Agapanthus
Hyacinth	Buddleia
Iris	Cornflowers
Violets	(bunched)
(bunched)	

Violet, Lavender, or Purple

Delphinium	Ageratum	Chrysanthe-
Hyacinth	Buddleia	mum
Larkspur	Gladiolus	Dahlia
Lilac	Petunia	Gladiolus
Ranunculus	Stock	
Rhododendron	Zinnia	
Tulip		
Violets		
(bunched)		

Yellow

Calla lily	Auratum lily	Chrysanthe-	Chrysanthe-
Daffodil	Coxcomb	mum	mum
Day lily	Marigold	Coxcomb	Rose
Hyacinth	Rose	Dahlia	
Iris	Snapdragon	Gladiolus	
Ranunculus	Tritoma	Rose	
Rose	Zinnia		
Tulip			

Orange

SPRING	SUMMER	AUTUMN	WINTER
Day lily	Auratum lily	Chrysanthe-	Chrysanthe-
Rose	Butterfly weed	mum	mum
Tulip	Coxcomb	Coxcomb	Rose
	Marigold	Dahlia	
		Marigold	

When planning the flowers to be used in a sanctuary, it is helpful to know which flowers and foliage have good keeping qualities, as well as their colors and the time of year they are most plentiful.

There is practically no flower that a florist cannot obtain at any time during the year, but the following are generally available flowers which do not have to be specially ordered and are the best buys.

SPRING	SUMMER	AUTUMN	WINTER
Anenome	Carnation	Camellia	Calla lily
Calla lily	Coxcomb	Carnation	Carnation
Camellia	Cornflower	Chrysanthe-	Chrysanthe-
Carnation	Gladiolus	mum	mum
Chrysanthe-	Rose	Gardenia	Cyclamen
mum	Shasta daisy	Gladiolus	Gardenia
Daffodil	Snapdragon	Rose	Gladiolus
Delphinium	Stock	Snapdragon	Iris
Gladiolus	Zinnia		Poinsettia
Hyacinth			Rose
Iris			Stock
Lilac			
Madonna lily			
Peony			
Ranunculus			
Rose			
Stock			
Tulip			

Color Symbolism

The symbolism of color had an early place in liturgical worship, due in most part to miracle plays which had to be easily understood by their audiences. Black was the dress of evil; white, the costume of saints. Red represented the blood of martyrs, and green, their hope of eternal life.

Much of the color symbolism understood and stressed by the ecclesiastics of the Middle Ages disappeared, however, in the Renaissance. Artists of this period doing religious themes selected colors for their brilliance and richness rather than for any liturgical association.

At the time of the Reformation, Protestantism, with the exception of the Lutheran Church, abandoned the traditions of color in favor of more freedom in expression and style of worship. Since 1900 there has been a new and widespread interest in the revival of liturgical worship, which is gradually being followed more carefully.

Today colors have the following liturgical symbolism:

White. Light, purity, and innocence.

Red. Fire and divine love.

Blue. Truth, constancy, and fidelity (rarely used).

Violet. Love and truth, or passion and suffering.

Green. Hope and an expression of quiet.

Black. Darkness, solemnity, and death.

In the history of the Church yellow and orange have never been recognized as liturgical colors, but flowers of these hues may often be used to advantage, especially with a green frontal.

Flowers Suitable for Church Decoration According to Color

White

Amaryllis	Chrysanthe-	Stock	Ismene
Anemone	mum	Foxglove	Larkspur
Aster	Clove pinks	Gardenia	Lilac
Azalea	(grouped)	Geranium	Lily (Madonna
Calla lily	Cyclamen	Gladiolus	and Aura-
Camellia	Daffodil	Hyacinth	tum)
Carnation	Dahlia	Hydrangea	Magnolia
Phlox	Daisy (Boston	Iris	Peony
Poinsettia	or Shasta)	Sweetpea	Petunia
Ranunculus	Delphinium	Sweet William	Yucca
Rhododendron	Rose	Tulip	Zinnia
	Scabiosa	Viburnum	
	Snapdragon		

Red

Amaryllis	Dahlia	Poinsettia	Zinnia
Anemone	Day lily	Ranunculus	
Azalea	Garden pink	Rhododendron	
Camellia	Geranium	Rose	
Canna	Gladiolus	Snapdragon	
Carnation	Peony	Sweet William	
Chrysanthe-	Petunia	Tulip	
mum			

PINK   OR   ROSE

Amaryllis	Coxcomb	Lilac	Scabiosa
Anemone	Cyclamen	Lily	Snapdragon
Aster	Dahlia	Magnolia	Stock
Azalea	Foxglove	Peony	Sweetpea
Calla lily	Geranium	Petunia	Sweet William
Camellia	Gladiolus	Phlox	Tulip
Canna	Hyacinth	Poinsettia	Zinnia
Carnation	Hydrangea	Ranunculus	
Chrysanthe-	Iris	Rhododendron	
mum	Larkspur	Rose	
Clove pink			

Violet, Blue, or Lavender

Agapanthus	Hydrangea	Ranunculus	Sweet William
Anemone	Iris	Rhododendron	Tulip
Azalea	Larkspur	Rose	Zinnia
Cornflower	Lilac	Scabiosa	
Dahlia	Lily (Marta-	Snapdragon	
Delphinium	gan)	Stock	
Hyacinth	Petunia	Sweetpea	
	Phlox		

Yellow

Calendula	Daffodil	Hyacinth	Snapdragon
Calla lily	Dahlia	Iris	Tritoma
Canna	Daisy	Lily	Tulip
Carnation	Foxglove	Marigold	Zinnia
Chrysanthe-	Gladiolus	Ranunculus	
mum	Goldenrod	Rose	
Coxcomb			

Orange

Butterfly weed	Dahlia	Rose	Zinnia
Calendula	Gladiolus	Tithonia	
Chrysanthe-	Lily	Tritoma	
mum	Ranunculus	Tulip	
Coxcomb			

Legendary Symbolism of Flowers

The symbolism of flowers in art has varied with the climate in different countries. From the first, artists painted what they saw around them. Exotic plants were never used because they were rarely seen. The pomegranate and olive, for example, were extensively depicted in Italy but not in the Netherlands. We find the columbine and the lily of the valley in German art but not in the art of Spain.

In some countries the artists did not paint plants with great accuracy; they showed so few botanical details that it is difficult today to identify varieties. This is especially true of the Spanish artists. On the other hand, artists of the Netherlands were meticulous in the use of realistic detail. In England symbolism was used on churches or buildings according to the fancy of the architect or stone-cutter.

Flower symbolism in art was already widespread in the fourteenth century. One fine example of that century's art is the "Madonna and Child with Saints in the Enclosed Garden" by the Master of Flémalle at the National Gallery of Art in Washington, D. C. This painting is full of symbolism both in regard to plant and subject matter.

By the end of the fifteenth century artists had begun to paint flowers for their own sake rather than for their hidden meanings. In the sixteenth century flowers were used solely as decorations in paintings, with the exception of the rose, lily, olive branch, and palm.

Flowers continued to be objects of art into the nineteenth century, when in England a revival of interest in mystical art restored their symbolism. Such men as Dante Gabriel Rossetti influenced religious sentiment by adopting the system of symbolism from painters who had preceded Raphael. The Englishman George Frederic Watts also made use of a symbolic style. Often, however, his meaning was obscure and not as precise as that of the great masters of past centuries. This revival was brief. With the rise of the impressionist and modern schools, the flower reverted to its role as an adornment in art.

If the symbolism of flowers were emphasized more today, arrangements in churches would afford greater interest and pleasure. Any study of symbolism is of certain value to members of a church altar guild.

The Lily

The lily's stalk is straight and upright; the plain and narrow leaves are almost austere in feeling. At the top of the long stalk is a cluster of flowers. Each is chalice-shaped, its perfume sweet and piercing and its form simple but noble in feeling. The petals are firm in texture and of a luminous white.

The lily has long been a Christian emblem. It did not appear in the Early Christian art of the catacombs, but when the twelfth century arrived, it was already the symbol of heavenly bliss. As its use spread, it became associated with the purity and perfection of the Virgin.

The Spanish were the first definitely to associate the merits of the lily with Christianity. The Spanish and Moors were fighting in the eleventh century. The Moslems instituted military orders called *rabitos,* whose members were vowed to perpetual warfare against the Christians. In 1043 Garcias of Navarre founded an order of chivalry sworn to service of the Virgin—the Order of the Lily of Navarre. The conservatism of churchmen and the tradition of Byzantine art kept lilies at the threshold of the Church until the Renaissance.

Since the twelfth century this flower has taken precedence in Christian art over every other growing thing. The lily of sacred art is *Lilium candidum,* which is supposedly a native of the Levant but spread with Roman civilization throughout Europe.

By the fifteenth century the lily was accepted widely throughout Christendom as the sole flower of the Virgin Mary—a mark of her spotless purity. On rare occasions when it was placed in the hands of the infant Christ, it became also the symbol of His perfect sinlessness. When we see the Christ portrayed offering a branch of lilies to a saint, we know that He is bestowing a gift of charity.

A more modern use of the lily is found in the fresco done by Lord Leighton for Lindhurst Church in England in 1864. This shows the wise and foolish virgins standing on either side of Christ, who holds a lily in His left hand. The lily here serves to emphasize the mystical character of divine nuptials.

The Rose

Among the Romans the rose was the symbol of victory, of triumphant love, and of the pride and pomp of life. It was also the flower of Venus. Because of its Greek and Roman associations the rose early was marked as a pagan flower; it appeared in Christian symbolism only after it was adopted as the emblem of martyrs. Hence, it became a sign of the triumphant entry of a departed soul into heaven, the sign of victory over the pagan. Since it had been the symbol of earthly love, it soon became the symbol of divine love.

Now the rose decorates our churches in paintings and in carvings of wood or stone, and in the embroidered vestments and altar frontals as representative of the love of God. Heaven is often painted as a rose garden, and the angels wear garlands and wreaths of roses.

A single rose, emblematic of heavenly joy, has long been the gift of popes to sovereigns, churches, or cities. It is solemnly blessed by the Pope on the fourth Sunday in Lent before it is sent to the recipient. This practice dates back to Gregory the Great (540-604) and has been an annual custom at the Vatican since 1366 in the reign of Urban V. Made of gold, the rose itself is a thing of beauty and fine workmanship.

In paintings the Virgin often wears a circle of red and

white roses, as a crown of serene joy, and many angels hold baskets of roses and carnations.

The Carnation

In early German devotional poems the carnation, or the pink or gillyflower, is occasionally used as a symbol of the Virgin. It is especially common in ecclesiastical art in Venice and northern Italy, where the rose might be expected. Symbolically the carnation is identical with the rose and may be interchanged with it. It often replaced the rose in Italian art because it was more abundant. The northern Italian artists probably preferred it because it was more precise in shape, neater in its habit of growth, and richer in color.

In southern France and Spain artists were more expressionistic and less accurate and so liked the elusive charms of the loosely petaled rose. The rose and carnation are rarely found in the same picture or sculpture.

The Olive

In Christian art the olive represents peace or reconcilation. It is first found in the catacombs in a painting of the mystic fish swimming toward the Cross with a sprig of olive in its mouth. The fish represents Christ who, searching for the Cross, brings peace to earth. The figure of the dove with an olive twig in its beak also is seen in many early Christian tombs. In the Old Testament the dove returned to Noah with an olive leaf as a sign that the wrath of God was appeased and that serenity had come over the earth.

The olive was the ancient symbol of peace. It is often used in illustrating Christ's life upon the earth. First, we find the Angel Gabriel bringing the Virgin a branch of olive as a token of his message of peace. Sometimes he is crowned with olive. The branch foreshadows the reconciliation between God and man which is to come by the Child, whose advent Gabriel announces.

In the catacombs the Virgin Mary is shown praying between two olive trees. After the twelfth century the Virgin is identified with wisdom and is eulogized in Ecclesiasticus 24:14 "a fine olive tree in the field."

The Spanish used the olive, but the Flemish neglected it. The German Martin Schongauver, a noted precursor of Dürer depicted the olive in his drawings and engravings. Because of its prevalence in southern Europe, the olive is used more by the Italians than anyone else.

The Passion Flower

The blue passion flower is symbolic in many ways. The leaves represent the head of the spear by which the Lord's side was pierced; the five stamens, the five wounds of Jesus on the Cross; the tendrils, the cords that bound Him; the ten petals, the ten faithful Apostles, omitting the one who denied Him (Peter) and the one who betrayed Him (Judas); the rays within the flower, the crown of thorns; the three styles, the nails. In the Catholic Church this flower is often used on Holy Thursday.

The Columbine

The graceful columbine is seen quite often in Italian art. It is used as the flower of the dove and as the sacred symbol of the Holy Ghost.

The columbine was originally connected with the seven Gifts of the Spirit. In Renaissance legend, these were Faith, Hope, Charity, Justice, Prudence, Temperance, and Strength.

After the sixteenth century the columbine was dropped from Christian symbolism and today it has lost its significance in religious art.

The Iris

Seldom used in Italy, the iris is first seen in the work of the early Flemish masters. The iris grew thickly around the dooryards of Jan van Eyck, Memling, and Roger van der Weyden and so was preferred by them. On the other hand, the lily was still exotic in Flanders and confined to some few convent gardens. Thus, the iris came to accompany and finally replace the white lily as the flower of the Virgin. It also became symbolic of the passion of Christ.

The Spanish adopted the iris as the royal lily of the Virgin.

Later the Roman Catholic Church accepted the iris, and the altar frontals in St. Peter's in Rome bear a design in which the rose, the lily, and the iris are united.

Other Symbolic Plants

Apple and Gourd. Death and resurrection of Jesus.

Cedar tree (used in churches at Christmas). Fastness of faith—prosperity—long life.

Christmas Rose. This winter-blooming white rose grew abundantly on Mt. Helicon, the mythical home of Apollo and the Muses. Early Christians knew it too and adopted it as a holy symbol.

Clover. The Trinity.

Cockle. Noxious weed, which invades tilled fields and mingles with the grain. Symbolic of wickedness invading the good field of the righteous.

Cyclamen (white). Sorrow, because of its red center.

Cypress. Immortality. Since the leaves of the cypress fall in a gale of wind, it is also symbolic of the righteous man, who preserves his faith even at the cost of worldly riches and honors.

Dandelion. Bitter herb of the Passion.

Fern. Sincerity and frankness.

Gladiolus. The Incarnation, the Word made flesh.

Grapes. Sacrament of Holy Communion. Twelve bunches of grapes represent the twelve apostles.

Holly. Corruption of the word *holy*. The "Holy tree" was planted on sanctified grounds in ancient times. The barbs on the leaves were symbolic of the crown of thorns, and the berries of the drops of blood of our Lord's Passion.

Hyacinth. Power and Peace.

Ivy. Faithfulness and memory.

Lady bedstraw. Common name for a plant that legend says was mixed with straw in the Christ Child's manger.

Laurel. Reward and victory.

Lily of the valley. Humility—purity.

Oak. Strength—force—forgiveness and eternity.

Palm. Victory over death—triumphal entry and immortality.

Pansy (heart-shaped). Charity—the Trinity.

Pomegranate. The Church. Its many seeds represent the rapid spread of the Gospel.

Poppy. Christ's passion.

Snowdrop and Marigold. Blessed Virgin—symbolic of purity and truth.

Star of Bethlehem. Advent and Epiphany.

Thistle. The fall of man.

Water lily. Charity.

Wheat. The bread of the Eucharist.

Yew. Immortality.

Decorative Foliage

The following types of foliage are especially useful in arrangements because of their durability and visual size. Used with flowers or in some cases alone, they add beauty and variety to a decoration program.

Andromeda	Dracaena	Iris
Calla lily	Eucalyptus	Lemon leaves
Caladium	Ferns	Laurel
Camellia	Ilex (Holly)	Mahonia
Coleus	Hosta	Palm
Croton	Huckleberry	Pandanus
Dieffenbachia	Ivy	Rhododendron
Many house plants		

Foliage for Planters Which Thrive in a Subdued Light

Aglaonema simplex—Chinese evergreen
Aspidistra elatior—Cast-iron plant
Chlorophytum elatum—Dragon lily
Codiaeum variegatum—Croton
Crassula arborescens—Jade plant
Crassula argentea—French rubber plant
Dieffenbachia seguine—Dumb cane
Boston fern and other varieties of fern
Fatshederalizei
Ficus elastica—Rubber plant
Ficus lyrata—Fiddleleaf fig
Ficus pumila—Creeping fig
Hedera helix—English ivy
Monstera deliciosa—Swiss cheese plant
Nephthytis afzeli—African evergreen
Palms in variety
Pandanus veitchi
Philodendron cordatum
Sansevieria in variety
Tolmiea menziesi
Tradescantia fluminensis—Wandering Jew
Zebrina pendula—Purple wandering Jew

IV

Whatsoever Ye Do, Do All to the Glory of God

(I Cor. 10:31)

Equipment and Its Use

The flower arranger should be familiar with all mechanical aids of her craft. Without good workmanship, which includes a knowledge of these aids, any arrangement loses much of its original intent. Equally important is the way the flowers are placed in the container and how they are held in position.

The following equipment is necessary to have on hand for church arrangements.

1. The yardstick.

It can be a folding one or a steel tape. The yardstick is of first importance in any church arrangement, since the arrangement *must* be the correct height and width for the

49

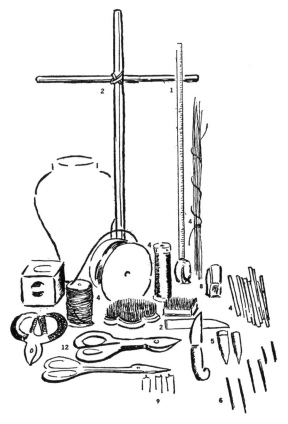

Essential Equipment for the Arranger. Each item is numbered according to the text: 1. Yardstick, 2. Needleholders, 3. A frame, 4. Tying materials—wire, thread, Twist-ems, 5. Waterpicks, 6. Floral tape, 8. Scotch tape, 9. Hairpins, 12. Wire clippers, scissors, and shears

space it will occupy. Whether the flowers are in a pair of vases or a single container on the retable, care must be taken that the tallest ones are no higher than the arms of the Cross. The space from the arms of the Cross to its base is the only area in which the arrangement can stand.

A note should be made of this distance, to be kept for

future reference. Even so, each new arrangement should be checked against the height that has been recorded as correct. The width of the arrangement also should be carefully checked so that flowers or foliage will not cover any of the upper portion of the Cross, nor be dangerously close to the candles. Foliage should never protrude so far forward as to interfere with the priest's or the minister's services. If the arrangement is well designed and of correct proportion, it will not dominate the Cross, but will rather enhance it. Too often one is conscious of poor arrangements which, being out of scale and lacking design, center interest upon themselves instead of on the Cross.

2. *Needleholders, chicken wire, and Sno-Pak.*

All three of these aids are useful in containers. The needleholders are especially so if the necks of the containers are large enough to admit them. Four small pellets of clay placed equidistant on the bottom of the needleholder will hold it firmly on the container's bottom and in position for the flower stems pushed down from the top. The vase, the needleholder, and the clay must all be thoroughly dry.

If the container will not accommodate a needleholder, the arranger may crumple chicken wire and push it into the vase. The wire must come high enough in the container so that the flower stems will stand in the mesh.

Even smaller containers can be filled with Sno-Pak. This is a white, flaked substance that absorbs water. Sno-Pak may be placed in any vessel, large or small, and mixed with as much water as it will take before being tightly packed.

3. *The frame.*

No large mass arrangements should be attempted without constructing a frame. This frame is always in the form of a cross. The best frames are made from bamboo stakes, tied securely to each other. The lower end may be secured in the container by a needleholder or by chicken wire. After being placed in the container this vertical piece should be one-half inch less than the desired height of the arrangement. Similarly, the horizontal arm should also be one-half inch less than the desired width when finished. (See diagram.)

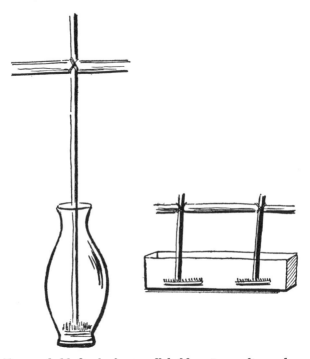

Frames held firmly by needleholders in readiness for a vertical and a horizontal design

Foliage stems are then tied to this frame. The central piece of plant material is fastened to the upright cane and the stems of the side foliage to the cross piece. When a substantial background has been provided, some of the flowers with heavy heads may then be tied on, and the arrangement is thereafter built up.

vegetables form a triangular composition. The skillful grouping of forms and colors create a distinctive design which is effective from a distance. A backing of magnolia foliage helps to unite the composite parts into a pleasing whole. (See drawing, page 94 for mechanics.)

Arrangement by Francis Patteson-Knight

Photograph by Mary St. Claire Weeks

Photograph by R. C. Wil

Presbyterian Church, Lookout Mountain, Tennessee decorated for a Christmas weddin
Oval shaped floral pieces of white gladiolus tie in with the design of the arch above t
Cross. Masses of variegated holly are used with the candles.

angement by Margaret St. Claire   Photograph by William J. Dempsey

mmer arrangement of yellow roses with their own foliage at Chevy Chase Baptist urch (Northern), Washington, D. C. This is a simple and effective arrangement thin a very small space. White petunias with their own foliage or white azaleas would ow to advantage in this type of setting.

Arrangement by Francis Patteson-Knight and Margaret St. Claire   Photograph by Charles Bap

Christmas arrangment in St. Clement's Church (Episcopal), Alexandria, Virginia.
a modern church with ceiling lighting and a center altar, a pair of stylized green agath
trees trimmed on both sides with a central panel of gilded fruit seemed most effectiv
As a substitute foliage, camellia or *Ligustrum lucidum* could cover the tree frames.

Sabbath arrangement at the Washington Hebrew Congregation, Washington, D. C. Magnolia foliage, white chrysanthemums, and white gladioli are arranged in the stands. The combination of cut flowers used with planters filled with green plants enframe the Tablets and help to maintain the center of interest within the sanctuary.

Arrangement by Nosegay Florists, Washington, D. C.

Photograph by Charles Baptie

Photograph by R. C. Wilson

Detail of a wedding arrangement in the Chapel of the First Presbyterian Church, Chattanooga, Tennessee. This is a well balanced design using smilax and white chrysanthemums. The candles are part of the design and give the needed height at both sides. The simple grouping of the chrysanthemums on pedestals adds drama to the scheme. The Cross remains dominant.

Lookout Mountain Baptist Church (Southern), Lookout Mountain, Tennessee. White gladioli, chartreuse hydrangeas, and dark green leaves of palm and huckleberry have been skillfully arranged. Placed at the sides of the sanctuary, they break the strong horizontal line created by the dark hanging and give a unified feeling to the whole sanctuary. As a substitution pink double larkspur, pink peonies and magnolia would be effective.

Arrangement by
Mrs. A. C. Willingham

Flowers for a wedding, Mary Chapel, Nebraska Avenue, Washington, D. C. This altar is done in a dignified manner, using magnolia leaves, gladioli, roses, and fuji chrysanthemums. Chrysanthemums were also used in the bridesmaids' bouquets; thus a unified effect was achieved.

Arrangement by Francis Patteson-Knight

Photograph by Glogau

Photograph by William J. Dempsey

Shrine of the Most Blessed Sacrament (Roman Catholic), Chevy Chase, D. C. An arrangement of the "florist's dozen"—twelve pale pink gladioli without foliage. The flowers show up well against the damask dorsal.

Children's altar, Church of the Good Shepherd (Episcopal), Lookout Mountain, Tennessee. Huckleberry foliage is simply arranged with white shasta daisies. This is suitable for a small, plainly furnished chapel.

Photograph by R. C. Wilson

Arrangement by Mrs. Hugh Cary   Photograph by William J. Dempsey

A contemporary setting in Wesley Theological Chapel, Washington, D. C. In a contemporary church leaves that are clean cut in form are effective. The green values should be compatible.

nother design for the Wesley Theological hapel. For color in a contemporary church iis is an excellent example of a distinctive rangement. Canna foliage and flowers iuld be used instead of the amaryllis and leaves used here.

Arrangement by Mrs. Richard Mattingly
Photograph by William J. Dempsey

Arrangement suitable for a cathedral or large church. Plant material: green and white striped pandanus, stock, and calla lilies. As a substitute snapdragons, chrysanthemums, and yucca could be used. The placement of the two lower stalks of stock add distinction to an otherwise formal arrangement.

Arrangement by Margaret St. Claire
Photograph by Robert Hurwitz

Arrangement for a country church. Plant material: ferns, Dutch iris, tulips, and flowers from the beefsteak begonia. As a substitution roses, double petunias and perennial begonias, would go well together.

Arrangement by Margaret St. Claire
Photograph by Robert Hurwitz

Arrangement by Francis Patteson-Knight   Photograph by Mary St. Claire Weeks

Horizontal arrangement. Plant material: Rhododendron foliage and lilies. The simplicity of this arrangement gives it dignity. It demonstrates a skillful handling of a minimum amount of material. As a substitution *Viburnum rhytidophyllum* and day lilies may be satisfactory if the arrangement is to be used only for a morning service.

...tical design for a contemporary church. Plant material: ... foliage, hostea, and a cluster of elaeagnus. As another ...ice yucca, hydrangea foliage, and small ivy leaves ...uld be suitable.

Arrangement by Francis Patteson-Knight
Photograph by Mary St. Claire Weeks

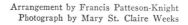

Children's Altar design, Washington Cathedral, Washington, D. C. Plant material: Sweet William, roses, freesias, and sweet gladioli. The plant material is in good scale for use in any small chapel.

Arrangement by Mrs. Herbert Bingham and Mrs. Frederick Reuter
Photograph by Mary St. Claire Weeks

Easter design. Plant material: Agatha foliage and Madonna lilies. Simplicity is the keynote to this arrangement. Camellia foliage with English laurel or *Ligustrum lucidum* may be substituted.

Arrangement by Margaret St. Claire
Photograph by Mary St. Claire Weeks

m Sunday arrangement, War Memo-
l, Washington Cathedral, Washington,
C. Plant material: palms. This is an
usual arrangement of great distinction.
is suitable for both Gothic or Renais-
ce as well as contemporary architec-
e. The containers used are the same
those in the drawing of the Easter ar-
gement on the title page.

Arrangement by Mrs. Hugh Cary
Photograph by Mary St. Claire Weeks

design which complements its ornate
e. Plant material: wheat, magnolia
ves, and snapdragons. Any small,
nted plant material may be substi-
ed in this arrangement if it is of a
or that will carry.

Arrangement by Mrs. J. C. Tobinson
Photograph by Robert Hurwitz

An informal summer arrangement. Pla[nt]
material: Queen Anne's lace and lili[es].
This is appropriate for a colonial chur[ch]
because of the fan-shape design whi[ch]
complements the architecture of the sa[nc]
tuary. Goldenrod and chrysanthemu[ms]
would be suitable for the same type [of]
arrangement.

Arrangement by Margaret St. Claire
Photograph by Mary St. Claire Weeks

Fall flowers. Plant material: yellow a[nd]
reddish brown oak leaves, green *Vib[ur]*
num rhytidophyllum, green arborvit[ae]
orange pyrancantha, yellow and r[ed]
chrysanthemums. This arrangement [is]
appropriate for a colonial church beca[use]
of the shape of the design and the ty[pe]
of container.

Arrangement by Mrs. Harry W. Harris
Photograph by Robert Hurwitz

vertical composition with fruit
nned for the same vase as the pho-
aphed Easter design). Plant mate-
agathis foliage, light green bananas,
apples, green grapes, and tiny green
Any fruit that is in scale may be
tituted, with ivy as the foliage.

Arrangement by Margaret St. Claire
Photograph by Mary St. Claire Weeks

t arranged horizontally. Plant mate-
mahonia, wheat, grapes, bananas,
s, and apples. This arrangement is
ble for a contemporary church. It
be used on a table in front of the
t, or a pair would be appropriate on
stals. A horizontal arrangement may
aced in many locations.

Arrangement by Margaret St. Claire
Photograph by Mary St. Claire Weeks

Photograph by Leet Bro

The church garden, Rosary Portico, Franciscan Monastery, Washington, D.
Trimmed boxwood placed in round planting holes adds interest to the paths.
simple beds are planted with hybrid roses and a boxwood edging. By the cha
door bearded iris, poppies, and other perennials flower throughout the season.

4. Tying materials—wire, thread, Twist-ems.

Wires should be neither too heavy nor too fine. It is wise to buy florist wires already cut, which are for sale in sizes 18 to 26. Spool wire is useful for wreath making and for hanging decorations at Christmas.

Green floral thread is preferred to wire by some arrangers. It is advisable always to have some on hand. Thread serves the purpose particularly well when tying smaller flowers together in bunches.

Twist-ems are valuable for tying stems to the frame, for assembling flowers, and for holding foliage together. They also have a special use as splints. Two Twist-ems placed on either side of a partially broken stem that the arranger wishes to save, and their ends bound with corsage tape, will preserve the stem for further use. Twist-ems may be bought in large rolls. On the market are new plastic ones which are re-usable and do not deteriorate as quickly as those covered with paper. When employing Twist-ems or wire to strengthen or lengthen a flower stem, apply them to both top and bottom to insure that the material will stay in place.

5. Waterpicks.

Waterpicks are used where short stem flowers are needed to fill spaces, but where the stem otherwise would be out of water. To use a waterpick, remove the rubber cap and fill the tube with water. Replace the rubber cap and push the stem of the flower through the hole into the waterpick. Waterpicks may be tied to floral picks or to a stem already in the arrangement to enhance the design.

6. Floral picks.

These are usually obtainable in several lengths. The square end should be pushed into the needleholder, and the pointed end is wired to either a waterpick or a flower

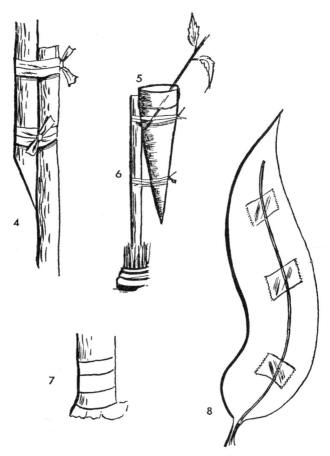

Equipment in use: 4. Twist-ems used to strengthen or lengthen a stem, 5. Water-pick attached to 6. floral pick, 7. Corsage tape wrapped around a stem end, 8. Scotch tape use to hold a leaf down or to coax it into a shape desired

stem. Floral picks are especially useful for holding heavy fruits together. In this instance more than one pick ought to be used. The result will be more substantial if the pointed ends are opposed in the paired fruits. Floral picks are also useful for holding medium-sized fruits securely to the platform.

7. Corsage tape.

Corsage tape is used to strengthen a stem. Hold a wire against the stem and stretch and wind the corsage tape around both stem and wire up to the flower head. On stems that tend to peel (like those of callas and tulips) the tape must be pulled and wrapped around the stem end. Green is the color most desired in corsage tape, but it is wise also to have on hand a small amount of brown and white.

8. Scotch tape.

This has several uses for the flower arranger. A leaf can be coaxed into shape by running a wire along its main rib and placing several short lengths of Scotch tape across the rib. Scotch tape can also hold a leaf down on a vase or fasten several surfaces together.

9. Hairpins.

Special hairpins suitable for arrangements are obtainable from florist supply stores. They are principally helpful in making wreaths and in pinning stems against fruits in harvest arrangements. Two or more hairpins are recommended where it is necessary to secure bunches of grapes to other fruits.

10. Cocktail picks.

Doubled-pointed, natural-colored cocktail picks are invaluable when using fruits for Thanksgiving or harvest festivals. They can be employed for impaling one small fruit upon another and in rounding off the form of a bunch of grapes. Inserting a pick into a single grape, lady apple, cranberry, or strawberry is one means of fastening it to larger fruit forms. The cocktail pick can also secure bananas to other parts of a fruit arrangement.

11. Oil.

Equipment in use: 9. Hairpins used to hold fruit and leaves in place. 10. Cocktail picks used to fill out shape of whole bunch of grapes.

Salad oil will shine up ivy leaves, magnolia leaves, etc. A small amount of oil poured on cotton and wiped on leaves improves the luster of any arrangement seen from a distance.

12. Clippers, scissors, and wire snips.

Good sharp scissors and clippers should be in every flower arranger's kit. Keep them clean and sharp. A sharp cut across flower stems preserves them and makes it easier to place them on the needleholder. Wire snips are a necessity if you wish to save your scissors when cutting copper or chicken wire.

13. Styrofoam.

Styrofoam is obtainable in both white and green. The 1' x 3' blocks are easily cut to any size or shape and make substantial bases or platforms on which fruit can be used alone or with flowers. The platform is placed on top of the vase or container extending the required width on all sides.

To give the platform stability, push two or more bamboo stakes into the vase from above so that they are inserted into the needleholder or through the Sno-Pak. Heavy fruit like pineapples may be held in place on the top of the protruding stakes. The arranger must make sure that the platform is secure before starting the arrangement. When using a combination of fruit and flowers, heavy stems may be pushed through the Styrofoam. In the case of more fragile stems a hole must first be made in the platform, or the stem will snap. Be sure to place enough water in the container so that all of the stems are in it.

14. Plastic covering.

Large pieces of plastic are very useful when making an arrangement. If one is spread out and the plant material and container placed upon it, there will be little difficulty in disposing of the debris when you are finished. The container may be carefully lifted, and the unused leaves or trimmings may be carried to the trash can intact. After emptying the plastic, make certain that it is thoroughly dried, neatly folded, and carefully put away for future use.

Smaller pieces may be useful when fruit arrangements are made. Place the covering around the arrangement so there will be no danger of any fruit's dropping onto the altar and causing a stain.

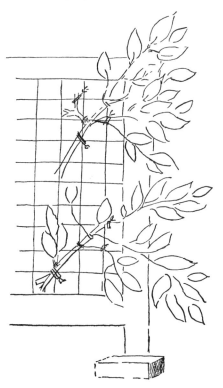

A screen is shown here with the first pieces of background material tied to it with floral tape. Bricks are handy to use in anchoring the composition.

15. Bricks.

A mesh net screen may be made to go behind a vase as a frame for an arrangement. This screen can be covered with greens. When it is placed on the retable behind the vase, it should be held in place with bricks painted the same color as the frame. If not, let them blend in with the retable.

16. Watering can.

Use a watering can with a long spout to add more water after the arrangement is in place.

Care of Flowers

Flowers and foliage for the sanctuary should be at the peak of perfection. Before making the arrangement, be certain that each flower and leaf has been examined for excellence in variety and shape. Those from the florist are already hardened; this means that the wholsaler or florist unpacks a shipment of flowers as soon as he receives it, recuts the stems, and places the bunches in a deep container of cold water. It is wise to strip the foliage from the stems of florist flowers and recut them on the diagonal so as to expose to the water as many cell tissues as possible. Any large leaves stripped off can be reserved for possible use later in the design.

Some foliage as well as stems needs to be immersed for two or three hours before being placed in a container. Calla leaves should be submerged in cold water for several hours, then wiped dry.

Flowers gathered from the garden can be hardened in the following way. For plants with a milky substance, such as poppies, the cut end of the stem should be burned immediately after cutting to stop the flow, and the stems should be immediately immersed in deep water. Woody stems like those of the lilac, on the other hand, should be crushed before steeping in water.

Flowers must have lasting qualities if they are to be on the altar for any length of time or if they are to be taken to the sick after the service. It is for this reason that gladioli, carnations, chrysanthemums, and snapdragons are most often used in altar arrangements. When there is to be an evening service, be sure the flowers used will not close up at night.

Certain flowers need a small amount of special attention. The stamens (yellow pollen bearers) of Madonna lilies should be removed to prevent them from falling and staining.

The green sheath from the top buds of gladiolus spikes should be removed so that the color will show, and the extremely tight buds at the top should be removed altogether.

Removing the tips of snapdragons will prolong the freshness of the flowers. The stems of certain flowers, such as the calla lilly, tend to split and curl back when cut. To avoid this, bind the stem about one-half inch above the cut end with florist tape.

When using fruits and vegetables, be certain that they are clean and fresh. It is advisable to shellac such fruits as grapes, pumpkins, or apples. In fact, it is wise to give a protective coating to all fruit that wilts quickly or attracts fruit flies. In arranging fruits or vegetables as in arranging flowers, it is important to have contrasts if the result is to be interesting and effective.

Scale and Proportion

Design is the blending of component parts of an arrangement into a satisfactory whole. Defined, design is no more than pattern delineation, involving a pure constructional plot or plan.

Selecting and arranging plant material has two aims: order and beauty. The arranger must keep these two goals uppermost and observe known principles for their attainment.

The most often confused of such principles are scale and proportion. Both are important in successful flower arranging.

Scale is the relationship between the sizes of the component parts of an arrangement. The relative sizes of the flowers as well as the relationship between the arrangement and the size of the area it decorates are both involved. A well-scaled arrangement for a smaller chapel would be based on Fashion roses rather than an amaryllis. Also, an amaryllis is much too large for a vertical container six inches in height.

Proportion is the size relationship of one portion of the arrangement to another. Remember that the visual weight of plant material has much to do with the height of an arrangement. Heavy material used in a ratio of one and a half to twice the height of the container is the general rule. Light, airy material may be from two and a half to three times the height of the container and still be in proper proportion. However, if the church is large, distance tends to make arrangements diminish in height. A better appearance is attained if the plant material is at least three times the height of the container.

Balance

Balance is another important principle, especially in church flower arranging, since the finished design must be firmly fixed. There are two types of balance. Symmetrical balance is the most common in churches. It is always quiet, dignified, and impressive, if sometimes static. This type of balance is achieved by placing an equal amount of plant material on both sides of an imaginary center line drawn through the middle of the plant material and container. Both sides are practically the same.

The second type of balance, and one more difficult to complete, is asymmetrical. This type relies on purely visual effects for its success. The two sides here may differ in form and color but have equal weight. At all times the

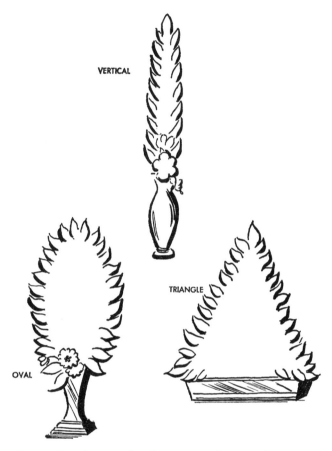

The oval and vertical schemes are best used in pairs
flanking the Cross, but the triangular design is effective
either paired or directly behind the altar Cross.

whole arrangement depends on the eye's measurement
and evaluation.

The three types of symmetrically balanced arrangements
most often seen in churches are (1) massed oval, (2)
massed triangle, and (3) massed vertical. The type of
arrangement to be used must depend on the architecture

of the church and the kind of reredos. With Gothic architecture, a vertical arrangement looks well. Baroque or Byzantine, on the other hand, calls for an oval or a triangle. In contemporary settings, a bold triangle or vertical arrangement looks best.

Under a suspended Cross a pair of balanced arrangements and a central arrangement can be combined effectively.

In a small church or a simple chapel a rather loose informal type of arrangement is suitable. A formal chapel demands a more tightly massed arrangement, yet one that should be kept dignified and simple.

If three arrangements are used, the center one should have balance within itself. The supporting sides will then balance one another. An excellent example of this employs

This fan-shape design used behind the Cross or as one of a pair is particularly suited for Colonial architecture. The horizontal massing shown here carries well in a contemporary setting. It may be used alone or in a pair.

a symmetrical triangle arrangement in the center with an asymmetrical right triangle or verticle one on either side.

The type of arrangement chosen will depend on the vases and on the space to be occupied by the flower arrangement as well as on the architectural lines of the church itself. Today much use is made of the long, low, planter type of container, which can be placed behind the Cross on the retable, or of a pair of planters on each side of the Cross. These are especially rewarding if the arrangement is low, for example, in front of a painted mural,

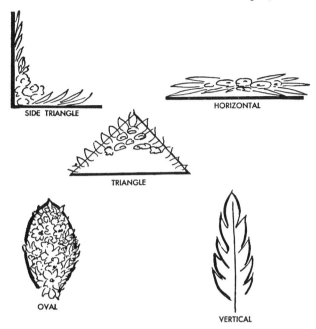

SIDE TRIANGLE

HORIZONTAL

TRIANGLE

OVAL

VERTICAL

The side triangle, horizontal, and full triangle schemes outlined here are intended for use in a long low planter. The oval and vertical schemes are most impressive in a Gothic setting where their lines repeat those of the architecture.

where tall arrangements detract from both the mural and themselves.

Color

The two best color schemes for church arrangements are: monochromatic and analogous. Monochromatic refers to the use of one color, its tints and tones. An analogous arrangement employs those colors that lie adjacent to each other on the color wheel with their various shades. To both you should add foliage in shades of green.

Some authorities hold that more than three colors may

be used in an analogous arrangement. In church work a more satisfying result can be obtained if the range is kept to three. The result is even more successful if all three colors are in the warm, or deep, range.

The warm, or advancing, colors include all shades of red, orange, and heavier yellows. Conversely, the cool, or receding, colors are green, blue, and violet. The lighter yellows can be used in both the warm and the cool color range. Either class has its uses in monochromatic or analogous arrangements. Of the two, though, the cool or receding tones are the least satisfactory, especially in larger sanctuaries. Cool colors lose a substantial amount of their eye appeal under artificial light. The unit of any arrangement, in fact, will change its tones when it is assembled under one lighting condition but is exhibited under another. No color is constant to itself, but is always subject to variation in different degrees of natural or artificial light.

A good analogous arrangement, therefore, will contain one of the more steady, more intense colors of the warm range. If composed solely of the receding tints, it will tend to wash out and become nondescript. A monochromatic arrangement of reds, yellows, or orange shades has the best chance of success, particularly in the subdued illumination of many churches. The best monochromatic design will use gradations of one color, with more or less of the darker or lighter values as the arranger wishes, but never in the same amount.

The carrying power of color is no more important in any flower arrangement than when in a church. It must first overcome the demands of distance, then lighting and background. Pastel shades will thin out and merge unless they are backed with greens. Blue and violet fade in the distance or become muddy under poor illumination. Almost nothing stands out against ornate or lavish decoration inside a church. This is why the altar, with its simplicity, is the best area for placing flowers and why, also, color in flowers is often needed to accent the plain cloths and simple fittings.

Sometimes light colors will succeed against a dark dorsal. They may also give a happy result if the chancel or the altar is a rigid white. Light flowers against a light background will show to advantage in a darkened church when they are framed in green. This will give them a dimension they would not have alone. Green, however, does not show up well in front of an altar curtain of dark cloth. Against its own shades or against purple or maroon, green loses visibility.

One color must always predominate; more than three used together require artful assembly. Too many colors establish a feeling of discord. This means that the flowers will not succeed in creating a logical and simple arrangement.

The exclusive use of green to decorate a church makes an effective display, but has its limitations. Planters look well, and, of course, so do palms and palm fronds. Palm Sunday, in fact, is one holiday for which a green motif might be planned. The altar can be backed with green foliage, but not covered with it. Green foliage lends itself well to vertical arrangements. Therefore, a little of it may be made to serve much, but this is often only possible in smaller sanctuaries.

The wise arranger, seeking harmony of colors in her decorations, will look about first at the altar frontal, the dorsal or reredos, the color of the walls, and the carpet. She consults the church's interior architecture before creating her own accent in the place. If the arrangements are for a feast or for a saint's day, thought must be given to the liturgical color. Also the availability of flowers at any time will determine the colors. The seasons put their penalties on the arranger as much as do the obstinate skills of her craft.

In Jewish synagogues we find elaborate use of flowers for special occasions, such as a wedding or a *bar mitzvah*. At other services there is a simple pair of arrangements or a single container such as might be found in any church with a central pulpit or a reading desk. The same rules and suggestions apply to these arrangements for color and form as to those for Protestant and Catholic churches.

Since there is no altar frontal whose colors change according to a liturgical calendar in the Jewish synagogue, no thought need be given to having certain colors for special occasions.

Also, in the Orthodox, Conservative, and Reform sanctuaries no particular color or flower is ever required. Whatever is seasonal and the most easily obtained may be used, provided it is suitable in scale and harmonious with the sanctuary décor.

Arranging Procedures

Having the necessary equipment assembled and with a clear mental picture of her goal, the arranger is ready for work. If her decorations are for a special religious festival or holiday, the head of the altar guild should have drawings posted of the arrangements desired. Generally, however, the arranger will make the choice and have the initiative of creating the holiday designs.

It is not always possible to have the right container. Too often the vases provided are in scale with neither the Cross nor the altar. Some vases have very small mouths, and others are not steady.

The ideal vase for church work has a good firm base and a wide mouth and is in good proportion to altar and Cross. It must also have good lines. Even a wobbly vase can be given some stability by putting shot, stones, or sand into the bottom before the needleholder.

There is a wide variety of suitable shapes for vases—the wide mouth and steady base are definite requirements.

Vases of silver, brass, wood, and pottery are all appropriate as long as they tie in with the general decoration. Alabaster containers may be used, but they discolor with water and often crack. To prevent this, line them with a thin film of paraffin wax before using them the first time. An alternative is to have a liner of tin made to fit the container.

Uniform papier-mâché pots are available and inexpensive. They can be used again and again. When properly banked and filled with flowers, they can be very effective.

Remember that a vase should be entirely dry before it is placed on the retable, to prevent disfiguring stains or rings of dampness. Use a soft cloth or a pair of soft loose gloves when transferring a finished container to the sanctuary. This will avoid fingerprints and the gradual wearing off of the protective lacquer.

The table on which the arranger works should not be too low. Almost without exception an altar arrangement will be viewed from below. If the arrangement is constructed while you are looking down on it, and is left unchanged at the altar, only distortion results. Also make certain there is enough room in which to work while fashioning the arrangement. Perspective is important for the finished product. The arranger cannot be so crowded in her working surroundings that she cannot step back now and then to get the proper angle on her work.

Sometimes the arrangement is partially made, then brought to the altar to be completed. In this process the arranger will need her plastic covering to protect the altar from water and to insure that all cuttings are taken away. Also all plant material and flowers to be used must be on hand at the beginning. They should be separated according to size and color. In this way the exact flower or piece of foliage needed is there, within reach, at the precise moment it meets the arranger's eye.

Before starting the arrangement, fasten the needleholder securely in the container and partially fill the vase with water. For church arrangements, it is important that the arranger first establish the outline of her design with green foliage or spiked forms. She has already taken careful note of the height and width limitations of the altar or sanctuary as well as of the church's décor. By the time she begins, she will have decided on the skeletal shape—whether the arrangement is to be spherical, triangular, vertical, or fan-shaped. Whichever shape is chosen, it must have solidity and strength if anything is to be built upon it. Firmness in an arrangement is another basic rule. Any shift in its design weakens and distorts its effect.

Sometimes the arranger may find it difficult to hold the outline materials and spikes in place when first putting them into the container. If so, she should cut two lengths from heavy pieces of plant material, such as gladiolus stems, a fraction longer than the diameter of the container's mouth. These pieces can be formed into a cross, their intersecting axis wrapped tightly with a Twist-em. By wedging this cross into the mouth of the vase, the arranger will create four openings to hold outline material upright where originally she had but one. A frame of bamboo stakes will stand straighter if this method is adopted to steady them in the vase. It also helps to press the ends of the stakes down upon a needleholder lodged in the bottom of the container.

After the outline is complete, the arranger selects from her material the flower that she wishes to place at the highest point on the frame. Often this flower will have a heavy head and must be securely fastened with wire or a Twist-em to the background material before she attaches other flowers. If the frame is triangular or fan-shaped, the flowers next added should be at the terminal ends of the triangle or on the lowest ends of the fan.

In using two containers, care must be taken that the stem lengths of all flowers are the same for the center and the terminal ends. Symmetry is imperative in paired compositions. A flower placed in the left lower corner of the left frame of one container must be immediately repeated in the right lower corner of the right frame of the other.

Creating a center of interest in the arrangement is the next step. This center must not be out of scale, nor should it comprise what is known as a "bull's-eye" in the design. Seen under poor light, some compositions with intensely dark flowers at their centers appear to have a hole in them. For this reason it is often easier to complete the center of interest toward the last, when it may be more effectively fashioned from the best flowers and its color relation may be gauged in respect to the surrounding material. The center of interest must harmonize in color, form, and texture with the rest, and light or dark should never dominate, but never disappear.

Dominance is an important structural feature. More than one form of flower is preferable. However, care must be taken that a single form predominates. Spikes, such as snapdragons or gladioli, should be used in a formal arrangement, along with such round forms as carnations or amaryllis. A different flower, if employed properly, can supply a satisfactory minor note.

One color must always predominate. Too many colors establish a feeling of discord.

Texture must be considered in planning a good arrangement. Texture refers to the roughness or the smoothness of the plant material. For example, magnolia leaves are smooth and shiny, while *Viburnum rhytidophyllum* (leatherleaf) is rough, much veined, and dulled.

A combination of textures makes a pleasing arrangement when the background material, such as pine, is enhanced by a small amount of smooth-textured foliage. Aucuba or ivy leaves are excellent for this purpose.

Never overcrowd the flowers. If sufficient flowers and foliage are used, they will hold each other in place. Too many flowers tend to disperse a design. Many arrangements have been ruined by one last flower that the arranger could not bear to waste. It is not necessary to stuff extra material in a vase to make the arrangement stand. But should there still be a feeling of instability after the design is completed, one additional means remains to give the whole the firmness desired. This is done by stripping extra stems of their foliage and inserting them in the container behind the outlining material. They can be pushed in unobtrusively, but their presence will give stability to the whole effect.

This stripping method is particularly helpful in vertical arrangements which must be kept narrow. Vertical arrangements, incidentally, are often the most successful, and they are currently the most popular in contemporary churches where more and more the experienced arranger has to work with bare, narrow altars. Generally vertical arrangements are more commensurate with the modern altar fixtures of today.

A vertical arrangement should not be wider than its container, though it is built up like any other design. The top flower is placed at the point desired. Thereafter, the arranger works down the spike or foliage framework, adding one flower at a time on either side of the central stem and keeping the design as narrow but as logical as possible.

Many times the arranger will be using church vases with narrow necks. These can accommodate flowers but seldom greens. You can add greens, however, by fastening them to a separate wire screen, which is in turn arranged firmly behind the vases. Care must be taken to employ only those greens that are long-lived out of water and whose leaves lie flat on the stem of the plant. Both huckleberry and lemon leaves are excellent for this purpose and are in good scale. Magnolia and rhododendron can also be used in this manner. The wise arranger will always save some foliage to use at the lip of a container, thus breaking the line of the vase at its rim.

When the arrangement is in place, fill the container with water.

When the flowers become withered, be sure to remove them from the altar immediately. Do not place the empty containers back on the altar after disposing of the flowers, but wash and dry them thoroughly and place them in a proper storage cupboard.

When completed, any arrangement should be viewed with a critical eye. It may need to have a leaf trimmed away or a flower lifted to improve the design. That which adds nothing to the finished product should be cut out or withdrawn. But first the arranger should hold her hand over the superfluous part to make sure it will not be missed. Conversely, the arranger may find that an additional flower or piece of foliage is necessary to fill a hole. Some other part can be shifted to justify its place in the design. The mass of an arrangement must never seem tight, nor should a vase be stuffed beyond its capacity.

As a final check, sit in the middle of the church and look at the arrangement. For a last moment assay its form and its relationship to the sanctuary and altar. In such a minute, a memory set, notes taken, will lay the groundwork for the plan, and the success, of the next arrangement.

V

That God In All Things May Be Glorified
(I Pet. 4:11)

Palm Sunday

During Lent, flowers are kept from the altars of some Protestant denominations, especially the Episcopal Church, and generally from those of the Roman Catholic Church. However, in *Matters Liturgical,* (see bibliography) it does state that flowers may be used by Catholics for an "extraordinary solemnity" and "on the fourth Sunday of Lent and on Holy Thursday." On Holy Thursday this is true only "for the Mass of the Christ and to the end of the Gloria of the Mass in Cena Dei." In certain High Episcopal churches flowers are used on the fourth Sunday in Lent.

Not until Palm Sunday is there new opportunity for arrangements in the sanctuary and chancel. Then, as this Sunday commemorates Christ's triumphal reception by the multitudes, palms and palm fronds only are specified. Roman Catholics permit the use of branches of palm, olive, or other trees during the blessing of the Palms on Palm Sunday. When flowers are permitted, the use of palms as a backing for them will help emphasize the symbolism of the day's celebration.

The limitation to one plant material will test the ingenuity of the arranger and make her resort to contrasts in size and variety to attain original effects. Such material, in fact, will be in short supply in all but a few parts of the country, and it will be hard to find.

Palm fronds, because of their relative scarcity, are not often seen, and they are difficult to arrange. The arranger who has a supply of them, however, and plenty of time may build them into flat decorations on boards covered with wire for use behind the Cross. They may also embellish window barriers.

Because of the scarcity of palms, more and more churches in modern times have marked the day with displays of potted palms on each side of the altar and altar steps. Other palms may be placed behind the choir stall, and two more at the entrance to the church as a reminder to entering worshipers of the sanctity of the day.

Care must be taken that there is nowhere a profusion or a density of palms. The pots of the palms should not be covered with paper, unless it is dull green to harmonize with the plant.

Easter Sunday

The sanctuary at Easter should be much more elaborate and glorious than on any other Sunday. This is the day on which the altar should project a feeling of gladness in response to the Resurrection.

Gold and white are the colors most frequently chosen. For this reason Madonna lilies are best, and are indeed the flowers most generally associated with the occasion. If the lilies are unavailable, however, or if their cost is a factor, other flowers may be substituted. Yellow roses or daffodils can provide the gold, while for white, azaleas, camellias, hyacinths, daffodils, tulips, or calla lilies are fresh and spring-like and are appropriate for the day. Arranged together, these flowers can give the altar an extraordinary effect of serenity. But the arranger will find that a combination of two colors requires more skill in order to prevent a feeling of spottiness.

Palms and palm fronds are also appropriate and traditional on Easter. As substitutes for them, the arranger may utilize lemon leaves, magnolia, huckleberry, and green privet. Potted palms can be employed forward in the church and principally in corners that would otherwise overshadow their decoration. It is wise, though, to keep potted palms quite far from the altar. Too close, they can interfere with and distract from the services.

Often at Easter an overdecorated church has the appearance of a florist shop. Rows of potted plants, especially lilies wrapped in foil with a large bow on each, lend a commercial air to the sanctuary that speaks of nothing but poor taste. Potted lilies, on the other hand, can be most skillfully employed, with or without palms, if their final effect is not too conspicuous. Papier-mâché containers are in good form and a new idea for these potted flowers. These containers are light and decorative enough to be taken to the sick after the services.

In the Victorian era large crosses and other religious symbols fashioned from wire and flowers were in wide

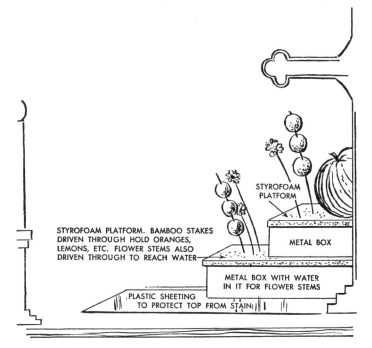

STYROFOAM PLATFORM

STYROFOAM PLATFORM. BAMBOO STAKES DRIVEN THROUGH HOLD ORANGES, LEMONS, ETC. FLOWER STEMS ALSO DRIVEN THROUGH TO REACH WATER

METAL BOX

METAL BOX WITH WATER IN IT FOR FLOWER STEMS

PLASTIC SHEETING TO PROTECT TOP FROM STAIN

Thanksgiving, the High Altar, Washington Cathedral, Washington, D. C. The mechanics behind the arrangement shown on the first page of photographs are revealed here.

favor. Their use is considered out of place and too garnish for modern arrangements.

Thanksgiving

Not all churches decorate their altars for Thanksgiving. Since it is an American occasion of gratitude and prayer, any decoration of the altar should represent the spirit and tradition of the day. This can be done with fall fruits and vegetables and with the colors of the dying year. Even so, it is wise to use restraint. An abundance of fruit and vegetables on the altar should not give the feeling of a produce store.

The plant material includes yellow and orange chrysanthemums, red and green grapes, bananas, oranges, lemons,
apples, limes, pumpkins, and wheat against a background
of magnolia foliage.

A dignified arrangement of fruits and vegetables is
always difficult to obtain. The arranger will find herself
challenged at the outset by varieties in form and tint, and
in shapes even among the same kind of fruit. Skillfully
handled, however, the result can be gratifying and have
exceptional success.

In small churches it is better to arrange no more than
three varieties of fruit in containers for Thanksgiving.
Pineapples and grapes with a few lady apples make a good

choice. A simple arrangement with chrysanthemums, with the accent of a few fruits or vegetables, also looks well.

In larger sanctuaries more variety in material is preferable. Greater freedom in arrangements is permitted. One that can be made to advantage is a triangular arrangement on either side of the Cross. Planters or tall vases are suitable in a large church, particularly if they have a good backing. Wheat stems show up effectively where the dorsal is dark in color. Greens are better for a backing if the dorsal or reredos is light-colored.

Fruits and vegetables which are appropriate and practical for use in Thanksgiving arrangements are listed below:

Apples	Peaches
Bananas	Pears
Cranberries	Peppers, red and green
Cucumbers	Pineapples
Eggplant	Pomegranates
Figs	Pumpkins
Lady apples	Quinces
Oranges	Strawberries
Osage oranges	Wheat

Christmas

Christmas (Christ's Mass) is liturgically the fourth-ranking festival of the Christian calendar. Easter, Whitsunday, and Epiphany supersede it, but universally Christmas has been the most popular and joyous. Ancient authorities have differed as to the date of the birth of Christ. However, that part of the early Church that adopted the so-called Latin rite decided that the most probable date of the Nativity was December 25.

The bestowing of gifts can be traced to the Roman custom of giving gifts on January 1; it is also a commemoration of the offerings of the Magi in Bethlehem. The yule log is a survival of the days of the Norsemen. The Druid ceremonies contributed holly, mistletoe, and evergreens. Many pagan customs have become added to the celebration through the years in symbolic observance of the day's hope—"and on earth peace, good will toward men."

Tradition dictates the use of broad-leaf or needled evergreens in the church on Christmas Day. Holly, either Chinese or English, is especially preferred. More recently this tradition has been extended to include poinsettias or, lacking them, a wealth of red flowers. Even so, white is still the sacred color of Christmas. No greater effect is needed that day than a white frontal and white flowers in white or gold vases beside gold candlesticks on the altar.

The choice of red or white flowers and of the number of containers depends on the arranger. Two vases should be sufficient, however. If other containers are desired, they may be placed at the altar ends or on pedestals at either side.

The choice between red and white flowers may also depend on the coloring of the dorsal or reredos. Red is complementary to and blends well with dark tan interiors. Any other color but white tends to thin out unless its mass is considerable. In larger sanctuaries this also is true of white flowers, unless they are built up and backed with evergreens.

Poinsettias, both white and red, are, of course, always outstanding. They may be cut and the stem ends burned to make them last in vases. Used in pots, poinsettias are more enduring and can be employed in mass. Single specimens in four-inch pots are the easiest size to work

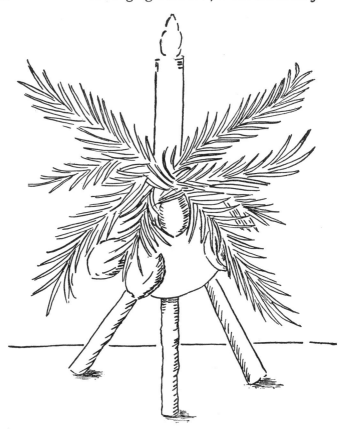

This ancient Welsh decoration is a unique and symbolic Christmas decoration. It can be paired with the Cross on the altar or used elsewhere in the church. The candle stands for the Light of the world; the evergreen yew twigs for everlasting life; the orange represents the universe and the nuts the fruits of the earth. The three logs on which the arrangement stands symbolize the Trinity.

with in a church of moderate size. Larger specimens will detract by their bulk from the dignity of the sanctuary and the altar.

Christmas roses and Star-of-Bethlehem make excellent choices for vases in a small, informal church or chapel.

Other choices at Christmas might be roses, gladioli, or carnations in either red or white. They can be arranged in a simple or an elaborate manner, depending on the style of the church and their cost.

The most suitable needled evergreens are white pine, cedar, Douglas fir, spruce, and arborvitae. In churches of modified Gothic architecture the cedar's shape conforms well with the pointed arches. Evergreens that are set against wooden paneling may be sprayed lightly with artificial snow to create a touch of winter inside the sanctuary. Trees inside the church are particularly effective if decorated only with this snow. It is not at all suitable, though, to attach religious objects, however symbolic, or Christmas baubles to these trees.

Some churches dedicate a corner or some other area to the representation of the Holy Family in Bethlehem at this time of year. In Roman Catholic churches the crib is an important feature and is always viewed with reverence and devotion. These scenes do not ordinarily lend themselves to flower decoration, and flowers in or around them may be out of proportion. Still, a deft backing of evergreen branches will separate them from the church fittings and give them a reality of their own.

Baptism

Baptism is a sacrament of ablution and serves as a means of church affiliation, a remission of sins, and a close communion with God.

Baptistries (from the Latin word for "place for baptisms") were at first sunken pools set into the floor, deriving from the sunken baths of Roman houses. Most of these were octagonal, sextagonal, or circular in shape and were generally surrounded by columns.

As more and more people joined the Church, Christian leaders found it necessary to build baptistries that were separate from the church. Notable examples are the baptistries of Ravenna and Florence.

By the ninth century infant baptism was commonly accepted, and as the practice of total immersion declined, the font inside the church replaced the separate baptistry. Fonts were initially constructed of stone and wood, later also of brass, copper, pewter, and brick. Today they may be cylindrical, rectangular, square, many-sided, or shaped like a caldron, and mounted on legs or a single supporting shaft. Some have the shape of a chalice.

When baptism is held at a font, a small amount of decorating may be done if space permits. Plants can be placed at the base of the font, but in such a way that they will not interfere with service. If the font is far enough from the wall, a pleasing effect results from putting flowering branches in containers on the floor or from arranging potted palms in the background. If there is a niche or shelf near by, an arrangement in keeping with the church's architecture may be placed on it. Generally speaking, however, unless the church is very large, too many flowers or palms will crowd the space behind the font. Above all, the font should not be used as a container for flowers. Nothing is more inappropriate.

There is no specific color for this occasion, but white would seem the most appropriate as it is symbolic of purity and innocence. Also it goes with any color scheme.

Confirmation

In the Roman Catholic Church confirmation is considered a sacrament, and white should be used on the altar. While confirmation is not a sacrament in Protestant churches, white is equally appropriate for the service. The altar frontal will be the color of the day if the church adheres strictly to liturgical colors. Against these colors, however, white is the best color of all, and the one most in sympathy with the event. Since white dresses are generally worn, white flowers are always in good taste.

Weddings

In decorating a church for a wedding, the arranger should aim to create harmony between the setting and the ceremony. At the same time, the very nature of the service will permit great freedom of arrangement. First, however, the family should discuss any plan with the head of the altar guild or, if the church has no altar guild or flower committee, with the minister. Many ministers have certain rules of their own on how and where flowers may be shown in the church; it is not enough to know what a particular religious denomination permits. Flower arrangements not cleared in advance sometimes will cause confusion at the last moment, making needless irritation prior to the ceremony.

When possible, have the attendants' bouquets harmonize with the flowers on the altar. This may be accomplished by matching colors or blossoms. It is equally important that the flowers do not clash with the dresses of the attendants. Consideration should be given to how the altar flowers will look with the dress colors once the attendants are standing near or within the chancel during the ceremony. A wise arranger will see that her decorations are a proper reflection of the wedding's theme and in consonance with it.

The type of wedding must be considered first in any decorating plan. If the wedding is formal and all participants are formally attired, calla lilies may be used for a beautiful effect. Conversely, calla lilies are out of place in a small rustic church with an informal feeling. Gladioli, snapdragons, or stock make interesting and informal arrangements.

Palms behind the chancel give the background a light airy feeling, which may also be created with apple, pear, or cherry blossoms. These, of course, must be in season. Flowering fruit branches are best with quite plain altar arrangements. Tulips, daffodils, or hyacinths are also good accents for these branches. An altar with a simple arrangement of magnolia or camellia foliage can be very striking.

At Christmas time it is appropriate to use cedar trees as a background. Seasonal flowers for the altar are the Helleborus (Christmas rose), poinsettias, roses, and gladioli.

Remember that the altar must be the focal point from every seat in the sanctuary as well as from the center aisle.

Do not put elaborate and gaudy decorations on the ends of the pews. White bows to designate family pews might include two or three flowers or a few greens. A small amount of philodendron or ivy trailing from the bow is effective and does not take the eye from the altar.

If candles are used at the end of the pews, they should not be lit until all guests are seated, and they should be extinguished before anyone departs. Be certain they are high enough that there is no danger of the bride's veil catching on fire.

To have a really effective color scheme, it is wiser to have all the attendants in the same color or in values of one color. In an all-white wedding green foliage is enough for the accent. This is especially true in the late spring or summer when dresses are of light, thin materials.

No matter what the color or type of arrangement on the altar, the same general rules follow for a wedding as for any other service in the church. Dignity is the prime requirement.

To have the church tastefully and artistically decorated does not necessarily involve a large amount of money. The following list of flowers obtainable from a florist is classified according to cost. It does not, however, include the many lovely garden flowers that may be used for either a simple church or home ceremony.

Spring

LESS EXPENSIVE	MORE EXPENSIVE
(Early Spring)	Calla lily
Carnation	Delphinium
Gladiolus	Easter lily
Pompon chrysanthemum	Gypsophila
Snapdragon	Imported lilac
(Late Spring)	Stock
Larkspur	White rose
Lilac	
Peony	
Tulip	

Summer

LESS EXPENSIVE	MORE EXPENSIVE
Carnation	Gypsophila
Gladiolus	Iris
Larkspur	Lupine
Snapdragon	Majestic daisy
	Marguerite daisy
	Sweet William

Autumn

LESS EXPENSIVE	MORE EXPENSIVE
Carnation	Fuji chrysanthemum
Chrysanthemum	Large chrysanthemum
Gladiolus	Snapdragon
Pompon chrysanthemum	Stock

Winter

LESS EXPENSIVE	MORE EXPENSIVE
Chrysanthemum	Carnation
Gladiolus	Fuji chrysanthemum
Pompon chrysanthemum	Gypsophila
Snapdragon	Poinsettia
	Roses

Funerals

Too often flowers are displayed with bad taste at a funeral. A profusion of floral tributes defeats the effect for which they were given. It is wiser to display only a few floral pieces in the church, so that the chancel is not cluttered and overcrowded.

In Roman Catholic funerals, no ornaments are on the altar, or, if they are, they are shrouded in penitential wrappings. A purple veil is before the tabernacle door. Around the coffin are black candlesticks—usually six in number. The coffin is placed before the altar just outside the chancel. The only flowers permitted in the sanctuary at this time are on the casket, and this use is discouraged. For a member of the military a flag may be draped, but a pall is preferable. If flowers are sent to the church for a funeral, they go immediately to the cemetery or are sent to hospitals. If the family expresses a desire for flowers to be sent to the sick, the funeral pieces are disassembled before sending. This is done, of course, by members of the altar guild. The flowers can be taken off the bases, and the Styrofoam kept for future use by the guild.

No flowers are used at funerals for those of the Conservative or Orthodox Jewish faith. Services are not held in the synagogue but at a funeral parlor, unless the deceased is an important rabbi. There are always two tall candlesticks, one at either end of the casket, with candles encircled with red glass. In the Reform Jewish Church a funeral may be held in the sanctuary or at a funeral home, according to the wishes of the family of the deceased. Flowers are generally placed on the casket, and sometimes two or three floral pieces are taken inside the funeral parlor. The rest remain in the outer hall.

White is the wisest choice for flowers on the altar. An alternative is to have the favorite flower of the deceased arranged simply on the altar. Never permit any floral pieces to be placed in front of the altar. Nor should the minister be hampered by a lavish display. Remember that a careful grouping of flowers according to color will produce a harmonious and effective unit.

Larger churches will often own and use a funeral pall. This is made of violet or black cloth, preferably velvet, and generally has a cross on it. This pall is placed on the casket when it is borne into the church. It is left there until the casket is removed from the sanctuary. The pall brings a single dignity to the ceremony and gives each casket an equality before God.

Children's Chapel

Many of the larger churches now have a small chapel for children. Here it is possible to hold short services for the children and, if an additional font is installed, to baptize infants.

Any such chapel will have its accouterments scaled down. The seats are small and a comfortable size for the youngsters.

In arranging flowers for a children's altar or chapel, care must be taken that they are in the right scale and in proportion to the Cross and the altar. Likewise, the size of the flowers must be harmonious with the limited space and the chapel fittings.

Special occasions demand that the decorations be in good taste and appropriate for the season. Portions of palms can be used, for example, on Palm Sunday. At Easter, Madonna lilies will be out of scale; small white roses, symbolic of the love of God, are a wise choice.

At Thanksgiving services make use of small fruits such as lady apples, figs, sickle pears, grapes, and bananas, which should be very small ones from the end of the stalk. Boxwood is always a good complement for fruits. Wheat stalks particularly blend well with fall vegetables.

For Christmas the Christmas rose is appropriate. If red is preferred, small roses may be used, or use white roses or a combination of the two. Small cone-shaped trees on either side of the Cross are also effective. These are constructed of boxwood on a frame of tapering wire and decorated with small fruits. Wreaths trimmed with the same fruits can be placed in the windows or on the door or doors.

A junior altar guild will stimulate interest in the appearance and significance of the altar. This group can be responsible for taking the flowers to the sick after the service. The members will see that vases are carefully washed, dried, and placed in a storage cupboard. From the adult guild they can learn what flowers are to be placed on the altar, and study the use of liturgical colors, their meaning, and the season of each. Another subject for instruction is the symbolism of the various flowers. From this experience, members of a junior guild can be prepared for other work in the future on behalf of the church.

VI

O, How Amiable Are Thy Tabernacles, O Lord of Hosts

(Ps. 84:1)

Permanent Green Plants

In many of the new churches and synagogues today, plant boxes or planters are becoming an important part of the decoration.

Two types of planters exist: one, designed by the architect, forms part of the permanent church furnishings; the other is available on the market and can be moved to various places to be used in a number of different ways. In both instances the planters or planter should be raised high enough to be clearly visible from any part of the sanctuary. A permanent planter should be at least twelve inches wide and eight inches deep (inside measurement). The planter itself may be constructed of stone, bronze, fiberglass, or wood painted to match the walls or trim. The front of the planter can be quite plain, paneled, or decorated with a simple motif. Overdecoration will detract from its contents.

Material for the planter is necessarily limited. To give satisfactory service it must first belong to a shade-tolerant group. Second, it cannot vary much in size. Preferably the plants themselves are set in their pots directly into the planter, which has been filled with peat moss. This procedure has several advantages. It makes it easier to change the pots from season to season or to replace a plant that is not doing well. It also obviates the necessity of obtaining soil in city areas, often difficult to find and hard to transport. Peat moss is clean, dry, and easy to handle. Once the peat moss is in the box, it should be kept moist. The potted plants should be watered whenever the soil appears dry on the surface. It is preferable to have liners for planters. Thought must also be given to the drainage of the permanent planter. It is important to the life of the plant that there is no surplus water in the bottom of the container.

On special occasions and for church festivals, flowering plants may be incorporated with the permanent greens. At Easter, for example, potted lilies, either the Madonna or calla lily, make an appropriate addition to the beauty of the service. White chrysanthemums or red or white poinsettias go well at Christmas. During the fall season, pots of chrysanthemums in various colors can give added interest to the boxes. The exhibition or pompon types are always obtainable, but at times the florist may be able to obtain the cascade or tree types to give variety.

The movable planter is usually narrower than the permanent one. An inside measurement of three and one-half inches wide and three inches deep is the usual size. These planters may be made of wood or of metal painted the color of the walls or trim. They may also be purchased in brass or fiberglass in various lengths. There are on the market metal ones painted black and the basket type, but the latter need liners. Movable planters are very satisfactory because there are so many places where they can be used.

Beautiful fan-shaped arrangements on the retable can replace ones generally done in vases. Again, small potted flowering plants—hyacinths, hydrangeas, daffodils, or tulips—can be knocked out of their pots and replanted in boxes behind any altar.

If a church has plain glass windows, the ledges of two or three windows on either side of the sanctuary may hold planters. Any arrangements in a window should follow its shape, especially at the top. Greens should be used to back and to frame window arrangements if they are placed against outside lights. Otherwise, the arrangements will appear sparse and unstable. If potted plants are used, it is easy to place additional pieces of the foliage in the soil of the pot to insure a substantial background. Some greens should be permitted to break the front rim of the container to give a softer and less rigid look. This applies equally to cut and potted material.

On Palm Sunday and Easter potted palms are appropriate. These are best rented from the florist.

Trees are used in the sanctuary only at the Christmas festival. Then cedar trees are best. If, in some areas they are difficult to obtain, another needled evergreen can be substituted. It should be of a good green and evenly branched. Care must be taken in placing these trees to be sure that they are secure and steady and will not fall and cause accidents.

Church Gardens

The exterior surroundings of the church should also be of great concern to any altar guild. With careful thought and planting, it is possible to augment the supply of flowers and green material for sanctuary decoration from the church grounds and gardens.

Shrubs and trees soften architectural lines and add greatly to the appearance of any building. When the shrubs are selected with the idea of supplying background materials for church arrangements, they serve a double and highly useful purpose.

It is best to leave the planning of the church grounds to a reliable landscape architect, who will suggest plants suited to the terrain and local climatic conditions. In some places, here and abroad, plants and trees are donated for church gardens as living memorials to departed loved ones. This practice is an important source of plant material. If members of the congregation can be persuaded to give living shrubs or trees to the church grounds as memorial gifts and if these are judiciously pruned at the right time, the clippings may be used in decorating within the church.

Church gardens have been in existence since the establishment of the early monasteries. The monks who tended them were among the first horticulturists, botanists, and men of medicine. Dioscorides, a Greek who lived in the first century A.D., wrote of some five hundred medical plants and was the accepted botanical authority throughout the Middle Ages. Many of the plants he listed were grown later in the Elizabethan knot garden and are found in the modern herb garden.

Today with the high cost and difficulty of obtaining skilled labor, a well-planned shrub border interplanted with flowering bulbs is both labor-saving and effective. The bulbs might include the daffodil, the lycoris, and any member of the lily family.

If space is available, a cutting garden of suitable annuals planted in rows is a help to those responsible for flowers within the church. If such garden cannot be on the church grounds, it is well to have it close by.

In rural and suburban areas, where there is more garden space, members of the congregation can be asked to donate flowers from their own yards for decoration of the sanctuary. It is often wise to set up a system of listing the flowers that may be expected to be in bloom at certain times and are readily available locally. Members should be asked to sign for the Sunday when they will be able to supply the flowers of a desired color and form. Often flowering branches, such as pear, peach, or cherry, are available from these sources, as are the lovely *Viburnum tomentosum* and *Viburnum carlesi.*

It has been the experience of many altar guilds that the cost of maintaining a cutting garden far exceeds a florist's bills. Even with successful gardens, florists will often be needed to supplement the supply.

The Bible Garden

This list of suggested plants for a Bible garden has been compiled by the Washington Cathedral's Cottage Herb Shop because of the large number of requests from other churches throughout the United States for a list of this kind. It originally appeared in the *Journal of the New York Botanical Garden* in March, 1941. A garden of these plants is an ambitious but certainly rewarding project.

Almonds—*Prunus* (*Amygdalus*) *communis*—Gen. 43:11.

Algum trees (juniper)—*Juniperus excelsa*—II Chron. 2:8.

Almug trees (rosewood or red sandalwood)—*Pterocarpus santalinus*—I Kings 10:11-12.

Aloes—*Aloe succotrina*—John 19:39.

Aloes (eaglewood)—*Aquilaria agallocha*—Ps. 45:8.

Anise (dill)—*Anethum graveolens*—Matt. 23:23.

Apple (apricot)—*Prunus armeniaca*—Song of Sol. 2.3.

Aspalathus—*Convolvulus floridus; C. scoparius*—Ecclus. 24:15.

Balm (balsam)—*Balanites aegyptiaca*—Jer. 8:22.

Balm (balsam)—*Commiphora opobalsamum*—Ezek. 27:17.

Barley—*Hordeum distichon*—Deut. 8:8.

Bdellium—*Commiphora africana; Balsamodendron africanum*—Gen. 2:12.

Beans—*Vicia faba; Faba vulgaris*—Ezek. 4:9.

Bitter herbs—*Cichorium endivia* (endive); *C. intybus* (chicory); *Taraxacum officinale* (dandelion); *Rumex acetosella* var. *multifidus* (sorrel)—Num. 9:11.

Box tree—*Buxus longifolia*—Isa. 41:19.

Briers—*Rubus sanctus and R. ulmifolius* (blackberries); *Solanum sanctum* and *S. sodomoeum* (nightshade)—Isa. 55:13.

Bulrushes (papyrus)—*Cyperus papyrus*—Exod. 2:3.

Burning bush (crimson-flowered mistletoe)—*Loranthus acaciae*—Exod. 3:2.

Calamus (sweet calamus, sweet cane)—*Andropogon aromaticus*—Song of Sol. 4:14.

Camphire (henna)—*Lawsonia inermis*—Song. of Sol. 4:13.

Cassia—*Cinnamomum cassia*—Ezek. 27:19.

Cassia (Indian orris)—*Saussurea lappa*—Ps. 45:8.

Cedar (juniper)—*Juniperus oxycedrus; J. phoenicia*—Num. 19.6.

Cedar of Lebanon—*Cedrus libani*—Ps. 92:12.

Chestnut (Oriental plane)—*Platanus orientalis*—Gen. 30:37.

Cinnamon—*Cinnamomum zeylanicum*—Song of Sol. 4:14.

Cockle—*Agrostemma githago* (corn cockle) or *Solanum incanum* (hoary nightshade)—Job 31:40.

Coriander—*Coriandrum sativum*—Exod. 16:31.

O, How Amiable Are Thy Tabernacles   113

Corn (wheat)—*Triticum aestivum*—Gen. 41:57.
Cotton—*Gossypium herbaceum*—Esther 1:5-6.
Cucumbers—*Cucumis sativus; C. chate*—Num. 11:5.
Cummin—*Cuminum cyminum*—Matt. 23:23.
Cypress—*Cupressus sempervirens* var. *horizontalis*—Ecclus. 50:10.
Desire (caper)—*Capparis sicula* or possibly *C. spinesa*—Eccles. 12:5.
Dove's dung (star-of-Bethlehem)—*Ornithogalum umbellatum*—II Kings 6:25.
Ebony—*Diospyros ebenaster; D. melanoxylon*—Ezek. 27:15.
Fig—*Ficus carica*—Prov. 27:18.
Fir (Aleppo pine)—*Pinus halepensis*—Isa. 37:24.
Fitches (fennel or nutmeg flower) *Nigella sativa*—Isa. 28:27.
Flax—*Linum usitatissimum*—Prov. 31:13 and 24.
Frankincense—*Boswellia serrata, B. thurifera,* or *B. carteri*—Song of Sol. 3:6.
Galbanum (a kind of fennel)—*Ferula galbaniflua*—Exod. 30:34.
Garlic—*Allium sativum; A. ascalonicum* (shallot)—Num. 11:5.
Gourd (castor bean)—*Citrullus colocynthis* or *Ricinus communis*—Jonah 4:6.
Green bay tree (sweet bay)—*Laurus nobilis*—Ps. 37:35.
Heath (savin juniper)—*Juniperus sabina*—Jer. 17:6.
Holm tree (mastic tree)—*Pistacia lentiscus*—Sus. 54 (Lentisk).
Husks (Carob-tree or St. John's bread)—*Ceratonia siliqua*—Luke 15:16.
Hyssop (reed)—*Holcus sorghum*—John 19:29.
Hyssop (marjoram)—*Origanum aegyptiacum*—I Kings 4:33.
Ivy—*Hedera helix*—II Macc. 6:7.
Judas tree—*Cercis siliquastrum*—Matt. 27:5.
Juniper (broom)—*Retama raetam*—I Kings 19:4.
Juniper roots—*Cynomorium coccineum*—Job 30:4.
Leeks—*Allium porrum; Trigonella foenum-graecum* (fenugreek)—Num. 11:5.
Lentils—*Lens esculenta*—Ezek. 4:9.
Lilies (iris)—*Iris palaestina*—Ecclus. 50:8.
Lilies (scarlet lily)—*Lilium chalcedonicum*—Song of Sol. 5:13.

Lilies of the field—*Anemone coronaria* (poppy or St. Brigid anemone) or *Anthemis palaestina*—Matt. 6:28.

Mallows—*Atriplex halimus;* also probably *A. dimorphostegia, A. tatarica,* and *A. rosa* (saltwort)—Job 30:4.

Manna (lichens)—*Lecanora esculenta; L. affinis*—(Nostoc) (an alga that appears on the surface of moist ground)—Exod. 16:14-15.

Manna (incense-producing plants)—*Tamarix mannifera* (tamarisk); *Alhagi maurorum* (camel thorn)—Bar. 1:10.

Melons—*Cucumis melo* (muskmelon); *Citrullus vulgaris* (watermelon)—Num. 11:5.

Mint—*Mentha longifolia; M. arvensis*—Matt. 23:23.

Mulberry (popular or aspen)—*Populus euphratica* or *P. tremula*—II Sam. 5:23.

Mustard—*Brassica nigra*—Mark 4:31-2.

Myrrh—*Commiphora* (*balsamodendron*) *myrrha; C. kataf*—Prov. 7:17 and Mark 15:23.

Myrrh—*Cistus villosus* (rock rose); C. salvifolius; *C. ladaniferus* (fragrant gum)—Gen. 37:25.

Myrtle—*Myrtus communis*—Zech. 1:8.

Nettles—*Urtica dioica* and *U. pilulifera;* also *Acanthus syraicus* or possibly *A. spinosus* (acanthus) and *Brassica arvensis* (charlock)—Prov. 24:31.

Nuts (walnut)—*Juglans regia*—Song of Sol. 6:11.

Nuts (pistachio)—*Pistacia vera*—Gen. 43:11.

Oak—*Quercus aegilops*—Isa. 44:14.

Oak—*Quercus coccifera; Q. lusitanica*—Zech. 11:2.

Oak—*Quercus pseudococcifera*—I Kings 13:14.

Oil tree (oleaster)—*Elaeagnus angustifolia*—Isa. 41:19.

Olive—*Olea europaea*—Deut. 28:40.

Onions—*Allium cepa*—Num. 11:5.

Onycha—*Cistus ladaniferus* (ladanum) or perhaps Styrax (benzoin)—Ecclus 24:15.

Palm (date palm)—*Phoenix dactylifera*—II Chron. 28:15.

Pannag (millet)—*Panicum miliaceum*—Ezek. 27:17.

Pine—*Pinus halepensis* var. *brutia;* also *P. pinea* (stone pine); *Abies cilicica* (Cilician fir); and *Juniperus drupacea* and *J. macrocarpa* (junipers)—Isa. 60:13.

Pomegranate—*Punica granatum*—Song of Sol. 4:13.

Poplar—*Populus alba*—Gen. 30:37.

Reed—*Holcus sorghum*—Mark 15:36.

Reed—*Arundo donax; Phragmites maximus*—Job 40:21.

Rie (rye or spelt)—*Triticum aestivum* var. *spelta*—Exod. 9:32.

Rolling thing (rose of Jericho, resurrection plant)—*Anastatica hierochuntina*—Isa. 17:13.

Rose (narcissus)—*Narcissus tazetta*—Isa. 35:1.

Rose (oleander)—*Nerium oleander*—Ecclus. 39:13.

Rose—*Rosa rhoenicia*—II Esd. 2:19.

Rose of Sharon (tulip)—*Tulipa montana* or *Rosa sharonensis* —Song of Sol. 2:1.

Rue—*Ruta graveolens*—Luke 11:42.

Rush—*Scirpus lacustris* or *Juncus effusus*—Job 8:11.

Saffron—*Crocus sativus*—Song of Sol. 4:14.

Scarlet (oak)—*Quercus coccifera*—Lev. 14:51.

Seven-branched candlestick (sage plant)—*Salvia judaica*— Exod. 37:18.

Shittim (shittah)—*Acacia seyal* or *A. tortilis*—Exod. 25:10.

Sope (soap made from the ashes of the burned roots of these plants)—*Salsola kali* (saltwort); *Salicornia fruticosa* (glass wort)—Jer. 2:22.

Spices—*Astragalus gummifer* and *A. tragacantha* are probably referred to, though many other plants with a pungent flavor may have been meant—Gen. 43:11.

Spikenard—*Nardostachys jatamansi*—Mark 14:3.

Stacte (sweet storax)—*Styrax officinalis*—Exod. 30:34.

Strange vine—*Ampelopsis; Vitus orientalis*—Jer. 2:21.

Sweet cane (sweet sugar cane)—*Saccharum officinarum*—Isa. 43:24.

Sycamine (black mulberry)—*Morus nigra*—Luke 17:6.

Sycamore—*Ficus sycomorus*—Ps. 78:47.

Tares (rye grass)—*Lolium temulentum*—Matt. 13:24-30.

Teil tree (turpentine tree)—*Pistacia terebinthus*—Isa. 6:13.

Thistles—*Carduus marianus; Silybum marianum* (holy thistle); also *Centaurea calcitrapa* and *C. verutum*—Hos. 10:8.

Thorn (Christ or Jerusalem thorn)—*Paliurus spina-christi*— Matt. 27:29.

Thorns (buckthorn)—*Rhamnus palaestina*—Prov. 15:19.

Thorns (jujubes)—*Zizyphus spina-christi; Z. vulgaris*—Matt. 7:16.

Thyine wood—*Tetraclinis articulata; Callitris quadrivalvis* (arar tree, an arborvitae relative)—Rev. 18:12.

Tree (tamarisk)—*Tamarix pentandra, T. tetragyna,* or *T. articulata*—I Sam. 22:6.

Vine—*Vitis vinifera*—Judg. 9:12-13.

Waterlily—*Nymphaea alba; N. lotus; N. caerulea*—I Kings 7:19, 22, and 26.

Weeds (seaweed)—*Zostera marina*—Jonah 2:5.

Wheat—*Triticum aestivum*—Judg. 6:11.

Willow—*Salix alba, S. cinerea, S. fragilis; S. Safsaf*—Isa. 44:4.

Willow (poplar)—*Populus euphratica*—Ps. 137:2.

Wormwood—*Artemisia judaica* or *A. arborescens*—Jer. 23:15.

Glossary

Alb. A white linen gown.

Altar. Place of sacrifice; Communion table.

Altar guild. A committee of women actively devoted to the service of the altar.

Altar rail. A railing placed between the choir and the sanctuary.

Almemar. The platform in a Jewish synagogue which bears the reading desk.

Antepedium. A hanging or screen placed before the altar frontal.

Ark. A chest in which are the two tables of stone with the Ten Commandments. It occupies the most sacred place in a Jewish sanctuary.

Baptistry. An area in which the baptismal font is located. In churches where immersion is practiced, the baptistry is a large tank.

Cantor. Singer of liturgical music in a synagogue.

Cassock. The black gown of the priest. It is the ordinary outer garb of a cleric and is not a vestment. It is worn outdoors in Catholic countries as well as indoors.

Cere cloth. One of three traditional cloths laid on top of the altar. This cloth is of waxed material designed to protect the fair linen from dampness or stain from the stone altar top.

Chalice. A cup used for the offering of wine to communicants.

Chancel. The altar end of the church.

Choir. A section of the chancel located between the nave and the sanctuary.

Communion table. In the true sense the table from which Holy Communion is served.

Crucifix. A cross with the Christ crucified upon it.

Dorsal. The curtain or hanging behind the Communion table or altar.

117

Glossary

118
Eucharistic lights. The candles placed at either end of the altar in the Episcopal Church.

Fair linen. The principal covering placed on the altar top. It should hang down on either side nearly to the floor. The fair linen is symbolic of the cloth used to wrap the body of Christ after it was taken from the Cross. It has five crosses worked on it, representing the wounds made by the spear and the nails.

Font. A receptacle of wood, metal or stone, used to hold the baptismal water.

Foot pace. The pavement or step before the altar.

Frontal or superfrontal. A hanging for the front of the altar.

Gradine. See Retable.

Lectern. The desk or stand on which the Bible is placed and from which the Scriptures are read.

Liturgical colors. Colors of the Christian year.

Liturgy. Church ritual.

Menorah. Seven branched candlestick, used in the Jewish religion.

Mensa. Top of the altar.

Narthex. The enclosed portion of the building at the rear of the church.

Nave. Central body of the church.

Office. An authorized form of service, such as morning prayer.

Pall. A cover for a coffin.

Paraments. The hangings and linens used in the sanctuary.

Predella. Step or base below the altar.

Protecting cloth. The cloth placed over the fair linen to protect it from dust and dirt.

Pulpit. A raised enclosed platform, with a desk from which the preacher delivers his sermon.

Rabbin. The name from the second to the thirteenth centuries for the chief authorities of the law and doctrine of the Jewish faith.

Reredos. The decorated panel behind the altar, usually made of wood or stone. It is often elaborate with sculpture, painting, or carving.

Retable or gradine. A shelf behind the altar on which the reredos rests. Flower arrangements are placed on the retable.

Riddles. Curtains at either side of the altar.

Sacristy. A place where the clergy may rest. Here the sacred vessels and vestments are kept secure.

Sanctuary. The sacred portion of the church which houses the altar.

Shavout. A Jewish festival which marks the end of the grain harvest.

Stole. A long, narrow scarf worn by the clergy over their vestments.

Succot. Thanksgiving week in ancient Palestine, observed after the fruit harvesting.

Sukkah. The booth made from tree branches as part of the celebration of the Jewish festival of Succot.

Surplice. A shortened tunic, usually of white linen.

Symbol. A visible sign to denote an abstract Christian truth.

Tabernacle. Name for the Jewish temple. Also a container for the consecrated Elements used in Communion services.

Transept or crossing. The area in the church between the choir and the nave, which in a cruciform-style church extends to the sides of the church, thus forming a cross.

Vestments. The ecclesiastical garments used by ministers in performing their sacred duties.

Bibliography

ABRAHAMS, ISRAEL. *Festival Studies*. New York: University Publishing Company, 1923.

ARMS, JOHN TAYLOR, and NOYES, DOROTHY. *Design in Flower Arrangement*. New York: The Macmillan Co., 1937.

ARNETT, DESSIE ASH; CLARK, LENACE ROBINETTE; and STEWART, BETTY ISAAC. *Methodist Altars*. Revised edition; no further information available.

BARRETT, W. A. *Flowers and Festivals*. New York: Pott and Amery, 1868.

BENZ, MORRIS. *Flowers, Their Creative Designs*. Houston: San Jacinto Publishing Co., 1952.

BERNSTEIN, M. *Color in Art and Daily Life*. New York: Robert M. McBride Co., Inc., 1928.

CAUDWELL, IRENE. *Flowers in Church*. Milwaukee: Morehouse Publishing Company, 1932.

CARPENTER, H. B. *Color*. London: B. T. Batsford, Ltd., 1933.

CHESKIN, LOUIS. *Colours and What They Can Do*. New York: Liveright Publishing Corp., 1954.

CLARKSON, ROSETTA E. *Green Enchantment*. New York: The Macmillan Co., 1940.

CONWAY, GREGORY. *Encyclopedia of Flower Arranging*. New York: Alfred A. Knopf, Inc., 1957.

DEARMER, PERCY. *Fifty Pictures of Gothic Altars*. London: Longmans, Green & Company, 1910.

———. *The Parson's Handbook*. London and New York: Humphrey Milford, 1931.

EDIDIN, BEN M. *Jewish Holidays and Festivals*. New York: Hebrew Publishing Co., 1940.

———. *Jewish Customs and Ceremonies*. New York: Hebrew Publishing Co., 1941.

FERGUSON, GEORGE. *Signs and Symbols in Christian Art.* New York: Oxford University Press, Inc., 1954.

FORT, MARIE JOHNSON. *Flower Arranging for All Occasions.* New York: Rinehart & Co., Inc., 1952.

GELDART, ERNEST. *Manual of Church Decoration and Symbolism.* London: A. R. Mowbray & Co., 1899.

GOLDSMITH, ELIZABETH. *Sacred Symbols in Art.* London and New York: G. P. Putnam's Sons, 1912.

GRAVES, MAITLAND. *The Art of Color and Design.* New York: McGraw-Hill Book Co., 1951.

HAIG, ELIZABETH. *The Floral Symbolism of the Great Masters.* New York: E. P. Dutton & Co., 1913.

HAUSEN, ANNA. *Arranging Church Flowers.* St. Joseph: Combe Printing Co., 1952.

HINE, MRS. WALTER R. *New Flower Arrangements.* London: Charles Scribner's Sons, 1936.

IDELSOHN, A. Z. *Ceremonies of Judaism.* Cincinnati: The National Federation of Temple Brotherhoods, 1929.

JONES, INA. *Arranging Church Flowers.* Dallas: Banks Upshaw & Company, 1950.

LUCKIESH, M. *Color and Colors.* New York: D. Van Nostrand Co., Inc., 1938.

McCLINTON, KATHERINE MORRISON. *Flower Arrangement in the Church.* New York: Morehouse-Gorham Co., 1954.

———. *The Changing Church.* New York: Morehouse-Gorham Co., 1957.

MARCUS, MARGARET FAIRBANKS. *Period Flower Arranging.* New York: M. Barrows & Co., Inc., 1952.

MOFFETT, OLETA STALEY. *Arranging Flowers for the Church.* Philadelphia: Muhlenberg Press, 1959.

MOLDENKE, DR. and MRS. HAROLD L. *Plants of the Bible.* New York: Stechert-Hafner, Inc., 1952.

REST, FREDERICK. *Our Christian Symbols.* Philadelphia: Christian Education Press, 1954.

ROCKWELL, F. F., and GRAYSON, ESTHER C. *The Complete Book of Flower Arranging.* New York: Doubleday & Company, Inc., 1947.

RUOSS, G. MARTIN. *An Altar Guild Workshop Prepared for Lutheran Churches.* Philadelphia: Muhlenberg Press, 1958.

SCHECTER, E. *Symbols and Ceremonies of the Jewish Home.* New York: Bloch Publishing Co., Inc., 1930.

SMART, REV. HENRY. *The Altar, its Ornaments and its Care.* Milwaukee: Morehouse Publishing Company, 1925.

STAFFORD, T. A. *Christian Symbolism in the Evangelical Churches.* New York: Abingdon Press, 1959.

SULLIVAN, JOHN F. *The Externals of the Catholic Church.* Revised by JOHN C. O'LEARY. New York: P. J. Kenedy & Sons, 1951.

VOGT, VON OGDEN. *Art and Religion.* Boston: Beacon Press, Inc., 1948.

WATKIN, WILLIAM WARD. *Planning and Building the Modern Church.* New York: F. W. Dodge Corporation, 1951.

WEBB, GEOFFREY F. *The Liturgical Altar.* London: Washbourne & Bogan, Ltd., 1933.

WEBBER, FREDERICK ROTH. *Church Symbolism.* Cleveland: J. H. Jansen, 1938.

WEIDMANN, REV. CARL F. *A Manual for Altar Guilds.* New York and Chicago: Ernest Kaufmann, Inc., 1941.

WHITE, E. A. *The Principles of Flower Arrangement.* New York: A. T. De La Mare Co., Inc., 1926.

WHITTEMORE, LEWIS BLISS. *Care of All the Churches.* Greenwich: The Seabury Press, Inc., 1955.

WILSON, ADELAIDE B. *Flower Arrangements for Churches.* New York: M. Barrows & Co., Inc., 1952.

WRIGHT, JOHN. *Some Notable Altars in the Church of England and the American Episcopal Church.* New York: The Macmillan Co., 1908.

WUEST, JOSEPH. *Matters Liturgical.* Translated by THOMAS W. MULLANEY. Rearranged and enlarged by WILLIAM T. BARRY. New York and Cincinnati, Frederick Pustet Co., Inc., 1956.

Index

123

ABOUT THE AUTHORS

Francis Patteson-Knight and Margaret St. Claire are both accredited flower show judges of the National Council of State Garden Clubs and the American Daffodil Society. Mrs. Patteson-Knight is a director of the American Horticultural Society and acts as an assistant editor of the *Gardeners Forum*. Both authors are actively engaged in church flower arrangement— Mrs. Patteson-Knight at the Washington Cathedral in Washington and Mrs. St. Claire in Bethesda, Maryland at the Concord Methodist Church.